IT TAKES A
GENTLEMAN
and a *Lady*

IT TAKES A
GENTLEMAN
and a *Lady*

The Old-Fashioned Etiquette of Falling in Love

ERIC LUDY

Ellerslie
PRESS
WINDSOR, COLORADO

Unless otherwise indicated Scripture quotations are taken from the King James Version®. Public Domain.

Passages marked NKJV are from: The Holy Bible, New King James Version (nkjv) © 1984 by Thomas Nelson, Inc.

ISBN 9781943592128 (paperback)
ISBN 9781943592210 (ebook)

ELLERSLIE PRESS
655 Southwood Lane
Windsor, CO 80550
Ellerslie.com

Published in the United States of America.
First Edition, 2015
Second Edition, 2016

EricLudy.com

CONTENTS

THE BACK STORY

As an author I have written far more words that were wadded up and thrown in the trashcan (proverbially speaking, of course) than I have written words that have actually been published. This is one of those works that ended up in the trash. But the difference about this work and the many others that were forever lost is someone dared to stick their hand into the trashcan and yank this one out.

I wrote this book in one week back in the spring of 2012. It was originally written on contract for inclusion in a movie. The reasons it didn't end up being utilized have been long since forgotten. But, long and short, it has been lost in digital no-man's-land for almost three years now, only to be recently discovered.

The book was originally penned under the title of "The Old-Fashioned Way." I love that title. But since Tyndale used that same title on the book that eventually was utilized for the movie, I veered away from that title for this book.

So, here it is. A new title on what is kind of an old book. It's sort of like climbing into grandmother's attic and finding an antique treasure. Even some of the illustrations are examples of that, as my children appear in their younger versions throughout the pages.

Maybe God's purpose for this book is that you would stumble upon it right now — and that it was written for such a time as this.

Loving the Old Way,

A WORD BEFORE

Hollywood would have us believe that physical beauty and sexual performance in the bedroom are the key ingredients to a romance that thrives. However, it's not "head-turners" that make their spouses happy for a lifetime, but rather those that learn how to turn a heart. And "heart-turning" is something anyone can learn to do.

I'll never forget when the cell phone first debuted on the social scene. My dad, the ultimate technological whiz, grabbed himself one of these babies and, with great pride, stashed it under his car seat. It was literally packaged in a brief case and must have weighed twenty pounds. I think he got the "sign-up-now-and-receive-the-$100-per-minute" calling plan. He was quite excited and, as a wide-eyed youngster, I have to admit — so was I.

Even to look at the thing now forces a laugh. In some regards it's even embarrassing to think I used to argue on the playground that my dad was better than their dad because he had this archaic contraption (which I'm not even sure he ever used) collecting dust beneath his car seat.

I'm guessing you probably noticed that this book includes the phrase "Old-Fashioned" in the sub-title. One of the concerns I think we need to address right up front is that this book isn't going to attempt to get you to trade in your new smart phone for some old dumb phone. This book isn't about digression from modern advances in technology to horse and buggy living. After all, I'll be the first one to admit that the modern rendition of air conditioning, toilets, refrigerators, and telephones are preferable to their predecessors. And, I personally wouldn't really want to read a book that told me to switch out my sanity for some clutzy old rendition of life.

I'm an old-fashioned sort of guy. And as I say that, my iPhone buzzes, my iPad bleeps, my MacBook dings, and I reach for my remote control and gently increase the volume of the music on my iPod in order to drown out all the techno-noises so I can focus on writing this paragraph. Now, where was I...?

Old-fashioned. Ah, yes.

I think most of us would agree that though we have modern convenience, modern technological wonders, and modern comforts — we are missing something. It's as if we left the restaurant and have that strange feeling that our wallet, our purse, our keys, our phone, or...hmmmm...something else seems to have been left behind. We pat our pockets, check our coat, and... hmmmm...it all seems to be there. But there is that strange sense. We can call it the hmmmm.

That hmmmm is in all of us to some degree. It's a notion that we've left something behind that once was ours. Or maybe it wasn't ours, but it was someone else's, and it could be ours if we just knew what it was. Hmmmm.

Well, if you checked out the subtitle to this book you would notice that we are not actually planning on talking about cell phones, but romance.

While out on that date with all your modern technology,

your modern techniques for sweettalk, your modern rendition for progressing a relationship physically... and fast — have you ever experienced the hmmmm?

Maybe you read an article in a men's magazine telling you the eight great ways to get a girl into bed on the first date, but as you get to the threshold of the hotel room, there is a brief pause. It's a wonder. A hmmmm.

Or, if you're the girl, maybe you heard some dating tips about the ten fool-proof ways to wrap this helpless man around your little finger. And yet, as you find him drooling at your feet, there is a flashing notion. It's a question. Is something missing? Is this what it is all about? It's a hmmmm.

There is something that has led you to pick up this book. My hunch is that it is the hmmmm. You see, you are not the only one with that little prick, that little wonder, that growing concern. There are loads of us out there.

The hmmmm is quite common.

I do believe we left something behind. And whereas our cell phone technology has progressed wonderfully, our love lives have not. You see, what we left behind doesn't effect technological development. Rather, it effects proper love development.

Most of us don't even realize we are missing something. But we can acknowledge that our love lives aren't working. We see the effects of broken relationships, bruised hearts, and shredded dreams. And as we progress down this prickly and painful road, the hmmmm has grown, the ache has increased.

So, what have we lost? Why is the hmmmm there? What is it that we are supposed to have in our possession and yet don't?

The answer to that question is a bit more complex than a simple pat phrase. But for the sake of this book, we can call it "The Old-Fashioned Etiquette of Romance." We are missing something that once was. Many people who have gone before us have tasted of its wonder and bliss. And even with all our technological advances, big screens, and big sound systems, we can't drown out the ache for something better, something more, something that has gone missing.

There is one key element of The Old-Fashioned Etiquette of Romance that I think needs to be laid out on the table and discussed first.

Hope.

In many ways, we've lost it. It was left behind in a previous generation. For it's a rare thing to find these days, especially when it comes to love and relationships.

We have become a generation of cynics. The experience of our parents' love stories have become the expectation of our own. Their divorce has suddenly become a premonition of our own future troubles. Or, for some of us, it's no longer a premonition but an unfortunate reality.

Many of us don't feel that there is a possibility of something better in the arena of romance. Oh, that's not to say that we don't want there to be something better; it's just that we don't believe there is anything better. We either feel our mistakes have been too pronounced, or that there just is no way our end result can change.

You may have the world's newest smart phone, but if you don't have hope, you are missing a key ingredient to a life that works and a love that succeeds.

This is what I mean by old-fashioned. I want to go back to the truths of yesteryear that once ruled in people's hearts and minds. I want to shed the postmodern mushy thinking of our day that sticks old virtues out on the curb with the trash. And I want to clean up those old virtues and put them back into prominent position within our lives.

So, what about hope?

To deal with the lost idea of hope, you have to deal with the lost idea of God. I realize that may be a bit overly metaphysical for some of you, but you simply can't have hope without including the only Source of it.

And if I were to be perfectly straightforward on this point, I would say what we left behind wasn't just hope, it wasn't just honorable behavior, it wasn't just a slower more guarded pace in love — it was God.

To be quite blunt, God invented love and relationships. They were His idea. And when we leave behind the Inventor, we will inevitably struggle in attempting to figure out how to fix the invention when it gets broken.

And the Inventor (a.k.a. God) is old-fashioned. But He's not old-fashioned like a twenty-pound cellular phone, a bouffant hairdo, or a rusty Ford. Rather, He's old-fashioned like honor and nobility; like knights and fair maidens; like chivalry and respect; like a handshake sealing a deal; like a man giving up his life to protect the purity of a woman; like a saved kiss, a white dress on a wedding day, and a happily-ever-after love story.

And in God's old-fashioned way, there is always hope.

God makes His knights in shining armor out of former scoundrels and His fair maidens out of ex-prostitutes. He builds chivalrous men out of once predatorial jerks and set apart women out of yesterday's everyday male-manipulators. He restores the beauty of a simple kiss to those who have lost all sense of the sacred. He makes those unqualified to wear white on their wedding day don the most sparkling snowy gowns. And He writes happily-ever-after stories for those wholly undeserving of His merciful attentions.

So, no matter your background as you stumble upon this book...this old-fashioned etiquette is just for you.

It's for all of us that have paused and let out a hmmmm within our souls. It's for those of us that have stopped at that threshold and have wondered if this animalistic, impulse-driven, spurn-all-that-is-sacred, reckless sexuality of our modern era is really the way to be going.

We, as humans, instinctively crave something more regal. In a sense, it's because we were built for something more. Like the throne of a king might feel if it were stored in a barn loft somewhere in Kansas collecting dust and buried under old boxes. We were built to house the nobility of the King of kings, to be His royal seat — and yet something has gone amiss. And there is a residue of longing within us. A deep abiding hmmmm.

In a sense, this book is about uncovering the dust-laden throne (which is us, lost in the barn loft) and laboring to present it, once again, to its rightful Master. It's about reclaiming sexuality as an instrument of true heavenly nobility. It's about men once again behaving as men ought to behave. And it's about women being transformed into truly feminine women.

But for this to happen, you have to open yourself up to hope. Without it, this book will be meaningless. I recognize that hope may have let you down in the past. But this is a different sort of hope that I'm encouraging you to foster. It's not hope in your own ability to finally turn the corner and behave like a gentleman or a lady. It's not hope in you, your stars, or your luck. It's hope in God's ability to be God in your life.

Follow your hunch. Follow that hmmmm inside. And let's explore an old-fashioned path that has fallen into obscurity in our modern time.

So, how does this book work?

This isn't one of those books to "finish." Rather this is a book to "soak in." These upcoming pages are crafted to introduce you to a new way of thinking, a new way of living. It's a journey into everything you always secretly wanted to be real, but didn't want to idiotically believe was possible if it actually wasn't.

I must forewarn you, though: it's a climb up the Mt. Everest of romance. It will be taxing at times and it may even get uncomfortable. The air is a little thin as you near the top and it will certainly prove your mettle. But the view is spectacular.

Consider me your friendly Sherpa guide. I know this mountain well and have spent a good portion of my life helping people, just like you, reach heights that they never before realized were possible.

This book is written to be a forty-day journey, but don't feel bad if it takes you eighty. The goal is not to conquer the upcoming pages, but to actually be impacted by what is in them.

This book is divided up into forty short meditations — forty nuggets of gold that, if understood and actually lived out, would not just alter your love life but the entirety of your life.

And I only have one small request of you as you embark

upon this grand journey into this old-fashioned etiquette of falling in love...

Please enjoy it.

Romance was never intended by God to be an academic subject, but rather a very real form of worship and praise.

So, without further ado, let's begin our forty-day journey.

WHAT EVER HAPPENED TO HAPPILY-EVER-AFTER?

"So, Eric, we hear you and Leslie are getting married? That's great! Congratulations! Just make sure you soak up the romance while you can — because once the honeymoon is over ... it's really over!"

From the day Leslie and I announced our engagement, we were showered with congratulations, best wishes ... and wet blankets. Plenty of well-meaning people did their best to prepare us for the "dismal reality" of marriage. We heard enough tales about stale romance, annoying habits, and insensitive marriage partners to last us well beyond our golden anniversary.

What ever happened to happily-ever-after?

It's been about six thousand years now since Adam and Eve first tied the proverbial knot and launched the marriage industry with an unceremonious market crash. That very first marriage didn't get off on the best footing with the snake and the apple and all. Add to that the eviction notice that soon followed and you'd have to wonder where the concept of "happily-ever-after" really came from.

Marriage has had bad publicity from the very start.

There are a lot of extremely dissatisfied customers when it comes to the marriage business. Very few married folk, or previously married folk, have glowing reviews about their stints as husband and wife. Most would tell you that the excitement they experienced during their honeymoon eroded hastily into a stale relationship marked by bickering and ever-growing resentment as the months and years passed.

The romance tanks, the sex dries up, he doesn't listen, she is a constant nag — the whole beautiful idea somehow loses its luster. The husbands grumble and the wives have nightly headaches, but they stick it out for eighteen more years "for the sake of the kids." This is the sickening reality of a majority of modern marriages — a sad soap opera of disillusionment and pain.

Not much of a sales pitch, huh?

Amazingly, we of the marrying age have spent a lifetime getting an earful of this "bad publicity" and yet we still desire to stand with our true love and declare "I do" in front of a church full of witnesses. We've heard these "marriage cynics'" complaints ad nauseum, we've witnessed marital trauma up close, and yet we still long to walk down the aisle.

Why?

Are we idiots? Emotionally blinded optimists?

Self-defeating masochists? A mixture of all three?

In spite of all the bad publicity marriage gets, there is something within us that wants to prove that the "divorce epidemic" won't strike our home. We believe we can do it differently than all those other miserable dolts who failed. We believe that we can figure out the secret to a lasting love story. We believe that marriage, if done right, is worth the outrageously huge risk of it all falling apart if it's not.

Marriage fascinates us — it woos us with its shimmer of possible beauty and its potential for "ride off into the sunset" satisfaction for a lifetime. Marriage has woven into its fabric the gold thread of something heavenly... if only we can figure it out and make it all work.

So despite the awful reviews by the multitudes of dissatisfied marriage customers, we press on, we propose, we set the date, we send out the invitations, we register, we book the church, we anticipate the day, we exchange the vows, we exchange the rings, we offer that kiss at the altar, and... we hope.

We hope that what we possess as a couple is a stronger variety of love than that which the millions of failed marriages before us possessed.

Those of us that refuse to surrender to the prophecy of marriage mediocrity — what will we find in the end? Will we find that taste of heaven on earth that we so desperately long for? Will we find the happily-ever-after romance that we've always dreamed of?

Well, that depends on the foundation we lay now — before we walk down that aisle. Just as the success of a farmer's crop is determined long before the harvest time arrives, so the ultimate success of our future marriages depends on the seeds we choose to plant in the springtime seasons of our relationship.

Beautiful lifelong romance is possible. It's God's design for a couple to thrive and only grow in their love and intimacy throughout their lifetime. But these kinds of love stories are rare, because the pattern by which they are built has fallen into obscurity.

In this little book, it is our desire to dust off the ancient way that God intended couples to discover the perfection of marriage intimacy. It's not by roses, rhymes, and tender rhetoric, or even by raw grit and determination. It's by allowing the Author of romance Himself to be your wedding planner.

day two

BEHOLDING
BEAUTY

Let me lay out my great concern over modern romance. It has no vision. Well, maybe I should say it this way: it has no lofty vision. Modern romance does have a vision; it's just that its vision is far too small.

Self-pleasure.

Yep. That's the grand vision of the modern lover.[1]

It sounds pretty pathetic when you just write it out like that and slap it on a page, doesn't it?

When we set our sights on such a minuscule end, we completely overlook the adventure, the beauty, and the stunning nobility of falling in love. All that God designed true romance to be simply gets thrown off to the side.

What if a man walking through the botanical gardens decided that his great vision was to get to the drinking

---

1 I'm working to reclaim the word "lover." Our sex-saturated culture has taken this word and attempted to make it something loose and sensual, when, in actuality, this is a word that should denote "one who loves well, with a heavenly variety of love." It should remind us of the notions of purity, selflessness, and noble kindness. So, throughout this book, when you see this word, please let the heavenly meaning of this powerful term press into your mind.

fountain on the north end of the lush, fragrant, flower-filled landscape? Suddenly all the beauty of a slow stroll through the gardens would be lost to him. He wouldn't notice the beauty, he wouldn't stop to observe the delicacy of the flowers, and he wouldn't appreciate the amazing fragrances along the way.

Sipping from a drinking fountain is certainly not a bad thing to do while at the lovely gardens, any more than human pleasure is incorrect in the romantic schematic. However, satiating human thirst becomes a bad thing when it becomes the sole focus. The greater glory of the process is forsaken, and the greater meaning is lost.

If the flowers are missed, the fragrance is ignored, and the cobblestone path is scuffed up in your whirling dervish to reach the water fountain, then there is a heavenly violation. There is a red bleeping light that should begin to go off in your soul. The reason that the cobblestone path was built in the first place wasn't so that it could get you to the water fountain, but so that it could slowly wind you through the enchanting beauty of the garden.

The same is true with the old-fashioned cobblestone path of falling in love. Its aim is not exotic pleasure in the bedroom — but rather, its aim is to see you fully come alive and reveal the marvelous things God can and will do in and through a man and a woman who trust Him with the pen to write their love story.

You see, this path was built by God, not merely to draw you closer to another human life, but to lead you closer to the One who created the very gardens you are walking in. And when you take note of the small things along the journey, and cherish them, something noble and other-worldly is allowed to enter your love story. And that something is, ahem, God. When you walk slowly down this trail rather than sprinting, you take in beauty that others around you will have completely overlooked in their haste. When you handle the flowers delicately rather than roughly, you will find that they grow more lovely. And when you take time to enjoy their fragrances, you will see that the fragrances increase with every passing day.

Now, if you are feeling a bit concerned about my shocking statement earlier that the cobblestone path of old-fashioned love is not primarily designed for your own personal gratification, let me clarify. If you walk this path correctly, there will undoubtedly be untold fulfillment and pleasure, just like there will certainly be a satisfying drink of water along the journey through the botanical gardens. But, if you make your ultimate vision the temporary satisfaction of your sexual thirst and selfish desires, you will have completely sabotaged the very purpose for which God brought you to this garden in the first place.

If self-satisfaction is your end, then you will never find the lasting satisfaction of true love and romance. You will merely be the depressed and forever-dissatisfied connoisseur of temporary, unfulfilling pleasures. But if you decide to let God take you by the hand and show you His amazing old-fashioned way, you will find pleasures beyond anything the Hollywood sizzle of our modern-era has ever dreamed about.

Here's to taking it slow and doing it right!

day three

WORLD-CLASS TASTE

Hollywood has thrown off the equilibrium of the entire system of love and relationships.

It has skewed everyone's tastes. And tastes are critical to cultivating exquisite love stories.

World-class chefs become "world-class" because they can discern the difference between celery and celeriac. They are snobbish regarding the ripeness of their vegetables — they are puritanical when it comes to their oils, their herbs, and their wines.

Let's just say that world-class chefs have world-class taste.

The same is true with world-class lovers.[2] They can discern between imbecilic and honorable. They are scrutinizing about the kind of person they will give their heart to. They are sticklers about character, purity, and

---

2 Just in case you missed my footnote in chapter two, I wanted to reiterate here that I'm reclaiming the word "lover" in this book. Though some have marred the beauty of this term, I'm determined to not lose its inherent purity and nobility. My use of it herein this book is the old-fashioned use, meaning "one who loves well, with a heavenly variety of love."

the reverence for God — both in their own life and in the life of a potential spouse.

Great lovers have great taste and refuse to accept cheap substitutes. The world-class chef only barbecues on fruitwoods and mesquite, while the world-class lover only proposes on full-confidence and plenty of prayer.

Hollywood has sabotaged everyone's sexual taste buds. It has painted hollow, low-class, perverted, self-serving men as the archetype male, while supplying visions of botoxed, half-starved, cosmetically-altered, and digitally-enhanced women as the must-get mistress.

It's like swapping out caviar for Spam.

When you marry one of these sad substitutes for true manhood and true femininity, you end up miserable.

Happily-ever-after starts with properly trained taste buds.

Men interested in one thing — yuck!

Men who speak with burps, scratches, and grunts — ugh!

Men who move too quickly — ick!

Men who have no idea how to protect a woman — blech!

Woman who are desperate — yech!

Woman who bare their souls without an ounce of discretion — yikes!

Women who manipulate men — red alert!

Women that gossip and tell tales on their friends — run!

I realize it would seem that I've disqualified 99% of the human race from the equation of your future love story. However, I would highly encourage you to not pine after the 99% like the rest of the rank and file masses. It's the 1% that have it together and thusly bear the testimony of great and lasting love.

So, you may be thinking, "Yeah, sure, I'll marry a

one-percenter." That's great. It shows excellence in romantic taste. However, don't think that a one-percenter is going to at all be interested in marrying you if you are one of the ninety-nine percenters.

If you wish to do this right, then you have to aim for excellence first and foremost in your own life. You must learn to be discriminating in your own soul. Your every word spoken should be examined. Your every thought should be monitored. Your every emotion should be guarded.

For some of you reading this, you probably need to start completely over in your idea of manhood and in your idea of femininity. You may have the Hollywood rendition of sexuality in your mind and it's cramping your ability to romantically succeed. You have a strut, a smolder, a swagger — and yet, a strut, smolder, and swagger won't help you love a woman well. You might have all the botoxed-beauty money can buy, but plastic, store-bought beauty doesn't translate into real-world intimacy, or truly knit you inextricably to a man in marriage.

If you are willing to get rid of the Spam and bring back the caviar, you've come to the right place. But make a decision now if you are interested in really doing this right. If so, no matter how bad your past is, you can have an amazing future. So, if you are game, it's time to swap out the drooling life for the daring life; the gossipy frivolity for the tamed tongue; the sexual duplicity for the loyalty of lasting friendship; the Hollywood-hyped erotic for the dignified, pure, and noble intimacy of trusting lovers.

I think it is probably a motto in heaven that the one-percenters have all the real, lasting fun.

Here's to refining our romantic taste buds!

THE MEASURING TAPE

If you ever saw the movie *Mary Poppins*, you would remember the infamous Poppins measuring tape that measured little Michael Banks and found him to be, and I quote, "extremely stubborn and suspicious."

Well, over the next four days we are going to be exploring the all-important theme of "relational readiness." And to do this, I'm going to whip out my own version of the "Poppins" measuring tape and stick it inside the text and stand you up next to it. After all, if you are not measuring well right now, then don't drag someone else into your life and punish them with your current issues. Instead of pursuing a relationship right now, you should be in a season of preparing for a relationship. If you have issues, then now is the time to get rid of them — not give them as a wedding gift to some poor unsuspecting soul.

Many of us are little "Michael Banks," who aren't measuring very high yet on the Poppins tape. We are demonstrating certain hazardous qualities that, if not altered, will pockmark our future marriage with certain inescapable problems. And, ironically, if these "hazardous qualities" were properly addressed now, prior to the commencement of a romance, they could be wholly eliminated.

I realize that the colors red, yellow, and green are rather kindergartener-level cliché, but for what it's worth I'm not attempting to sound smart in using them, but practical.

As my three-year-old daughter would say, "Daddy, red means stop." Please remember that simple rule of thumb, not just the next time you are out driving through town, but the entire while you are reading this book.

There is a Red Zone on the measuring tape of romantic assessment, and, to be quite frank, if you find that you, or the one you are considering pursuing, are showing signs of romantic underdevelopment, then note that red indicates stop. It certainly does not indicate that nothing good could ever come of it, but it does indicate that nothing good will come of it if it is pursued at this current time.

The Yellow Zone on the measuring tape means "slow and/or pause." If you, or someone else, is hovering in the yellow territory, that isn't necessarily a bad sign; it just means there is a bit more growth that is necessary prior to a green light. The active verbs in the yellow territory are wait, watch, and pray. Yellows are showing good signs of development, but, like a toddler, shouldn't be given keys to the gun cabinet quite yet. But, with a little time, they may prove to be a real catch.

The Green Zone is the indicator of basic readiness. It by no means should ever be interpreted to mean "finished product." It simply means "ready to take next steps forward and do it correctly."

No matter where you start out in your measurement, please don't let it define where you end up. Where you start is precisely that — a starting place. But may this book introduce you to the great Almighty God who takes underdeveloped, undernourished, pale-faced romantics and builds them into amazing pictures of His profound grace.

Here's to not ever pitching our tent, but pressing onward and upward ever after.

day five

THE RED ZONE

We have a problem of epidemic proportions nowadays. It's a problem with perspective. We are considering artificial implants to be beautiful, jerks to be debonaire, and one night stands to be the basis for a forever-kind-of-love.

I guess it makes sense. When you lose sight of the original, counterfeits can run free without scrutiny.

In many ways, we have lost sight of the original brand of romance. The sort of romance that is truly heavenly in all its deportment, pure in all its manner, and noble in all its behavior.

But, to get it back, we need to start getting tough on both ourselves and our standards for romantic readiness.

This is difficult, because in many ways we all are part of the very problem we are trying to solve. We personally have lived lower-class lives and thusly we have contributed to the lower-class view of romantic relationship.

So, if we are going to get serious about changing the direction of this whole ship, we need to start with ourselves.

This might be hard, but I'm going to ask you to not think about someone else as we bring out the measuring tape. I want you, first, to take a long, hard look at your own personal readiness.

The first question that really matters is, "Am I actually ready to love someone well?"

If the answer is "no," then it is far better to realize that now and actually do something about it, than bury your head in the sand and head straight over a cliff and crush two hearts in the process.

Let's do some soul-searching.

There are three glaring signs that show unreadiness for relationship. If you are showing even small hints of the following three signs, then it is highly possible you are measuring in the Red Zone.

No spiritual desire. If you are not showing signs of spiritual desire, a longing to know God, know His ways, or even have the craving to draw closer to your Creator, then something is amiss. I recognize that, as a result of this spiritual lassitude, you will likely not care a whit what I actually think on the matter. But nonetheless I want to go on record for declaring that divine disinterest does not bode well for your romantic future, unless something changes.

No drive for betterment. If you are not demonstrating eagerness for personal betterment — you don't really care about changing, of growing, of being further refined and polished — you are really quite satisfied with yourself, right where you are at — these are, again, not healthy signs. For what you are now is what you are going to bring to the relationship. And without a drive for betterment, there certainly will never be any improvement on what is currently hanging around inside your body.

No acceptance of change. If you are not wanting

to change the way in which you build your romantic relationships and you are convinced that your "self-first" approach to love, life, and the eternal is the way to go — then there is definitely a big red stop sign bleeping above your soul.

Do you match any of the above? Because, if so, I want you to know that as it currently stands you can technically enter into a relationship, but you are not going to have a good one. Relational success hinges on humble pliability to the Living God, who invented the opposite sex and invented the whole concept of relating with them.

Now, after you have spent ample time determining your own soul on the matter, it is also necessary that you inspect the other side of the relational equation. Is the person you are interested in showing signs of life, growth, and potential, or are you seeing a big red stop sign bleeping above their soul?

Remember, as my three-year-old says, "red means stop." And it means stop not just at traffic signals, but in the arena of love stories too.

Please note that stopping now does not mean that you might not have a green light someday in the future. It's that right now, either you or the person you are considering needs to do a little soul searching, praying, and crying out for God to intervene. A change of life is necessary. And I don't mean a few small alterations, but wholesale renovation — a liquidation of an old manner of living in exchange for an entirely new one.

When you are in the Red Zone, you need to be rescued from yourself, but the dilemma is you don't realize you need to be rescued. And that is your big problem. In order to be rescued, you need to know your dire need to be rescued. After all, who is going to allow someone to lay them flat on a stretcher, stick a breathing mask on their face, and throw them into a flight-for-life helicopter when they are convinced that they are perfectly healthy?

Simply put, if you are in the Red Zone, you still need to be altered by Jesus Christ. You have not yet recognized your need for rescue from your own sinful, selfish prerogative, and thusly you are not yet fit to be honorable and excellent in your future marriage.

I realize that sounds a bit too straightforward for our modern "all roads lead to God" taste buds, but, for the sake of your future love life, I'm giving it to you straight.

I recognize that you may already have slammed this book shut if you are measuring Red, but my encouragement to you is to keep reading. Hang in there. You may be upset with me right now, but if you catch this vision and recognize how truly beautiful it is to live the right way, you'll be happy that you hung around a little longer.

Here's a great prayer for you to pray:

God, if I'm in need of You, please somehow show me my need. If my heart is hard, please soften it. If my mind is closed to You and Your ways, please open it up.

I guarantee you that He most certainly will.

Here's to a spoonful of medicine without the sugar to help get it down.

day six

THE YELLOW ZONE

Contrary to popular opinion, biological age is not your criteria for determining if you or someone else is ready to advance a relationship. Just because you are fifty-five by no means should suggest that you are fit to succeed in the grand challenge of world-class romance.

In fact, age can sometimes be a cover for immaturity and unreadiness, because we all sort of assume that with age comes refinement. But refinement can only be worked in someone who is willingly accepting the refining work. And that is true for someone who is eighteen or eighty-eight.

Since most women have never seen a true gentleman, they can easily confuse ardor for honor. Don't be one of them. A man can say the right thing, but can he live the right thing out?

The sighting of one real gentleman can oftentimes solve this issue. If women could just see it, then maybe they wouldn't settle for such low-class idiocy nowadays.

Men are being duped the very same way. They are confusing external shapeliness for true behavioral beauty. A woman can look just right on the outside, and make your life miserable, 'til death do you part, on the inside.

Please take my advice and don't just say "yes" to the first person who asks you out, or, for that matter, the first person that asks you to marry them. Pause, evaluate, look them over.

It's not rude to be slow. Better put, it's stupid to be fast.

This is where the measurement comes into play.

For the sake of this book, I've broken down the concept of readiness into three "zones" of readiness: Red, Yellow, and Green. And like a measuring tape, I would like each of us to take our turn standing up next to them.

When someone is measuring in the Yellow Zone, that means they have caught the vision of honor and excellence. However, they are experiencing a difficulty in the proper implementation of this grand notion of heavenly living. They are trying, but they can't seem to stay in the saddle of this massive white, fire-breathing stallion known as perfect behavior. This is normal for each of us to spend a stretch of time in this Yellow hallway "trying our hearts out and failing daily," but it is important to note that you should not press forward in a serious relationship while either you or the one you are considering pursuing is still in the Yellow Zone.

Yellow indicates pause, watch, evaluate, and wait patiently. It demonstrates "virtue in the making."

When witnessing someone in the Yellow Zone, you are watching to see persistence and humility. Failure is a very familiar thing to the process of proper growth and development, but failure should never be justified or downplayed. It should be responded to with gritted-teeth-determination to see success the next go-around. So, when you, or someone you love, is walking through this, the true sign of health is that if they fail they get right back up, with a disgust for their mistake and a whole-hearted desire to do it 100% right from that point forward.

Yellows that persevere can't help but grow up and turn Green. They learn, and some learn more quickly than others, the secret of staying in the saddle. And truly, that is the key difference between Yellow and Green — a secret.

day seven

THE GREEN ZONE

Those measuring Green are merely past Reds changed into Yellows by the saving grace of Almighty God, who then matured into Greens in and through the same amazing grace being constantly and consistently applied to their lives. But Greens know something that Yellows don't. They know the secret of staying in the saddle and not getting bucked off the wild and powerful stallion known as perfect behavior.

The Green has realized that it is utterly impossible to stay in the saddle. Even God makes that clear. God says, "You can't do it." But the Green does not despair, because God also says, "And yet, you must do it." That seeming contradiction keeps the Young Yellows guessing for quite some time. But here's the great secret...

What is impossible with man IS possible with God.

You see, no one can possibly stay in the saddle of this mighty pure and holy stallion. The stallion's name is Perfect Righteousness. And he has tossed off every single man or woman that has ever climbed on his back throughout the ages. That is, all but One. For this stallion of perfect behavior has been ridden. In fact, two thousand years ago, it was done to the chagrin of all the powers of hell by a man named Jesus Christ. For in doing so, He made a way for us to now ride the stallion. And that is on His lap, in His arms, staying in His presence. By doing this, He saves us from the doldrums of everyday, mediocre human behavior and enables us to actually love and serve and give and care as He does — with heavenly behavior, and with heavenly honor.

The great secret to living as a Green — and truly being made ready to move forward into the depths of romantic love and intimacy — is getting up onto Jesus' lap while He rides the powerful and glorious stallion, and clinging to Him and remaining there every moment for the rest of your life, taking full advantage of His great and dexterous riding ability.

A Green is someone altered by Jesus Christ, and thusly, someone made ready to be excellent in marriage.

So be inspired. If you are a Red, why not let Jesus begin the process of rescue in your soul today? If you are a Yellow, ask God to teach you how to actually live this life instead of merely esteeming its grandeur — He will most certainly answer. And if you are a Green, praise God that He has laid such a foundation of strength in your life, and then subsequently honor Him by pressing forward into the depths of growth in Christ Jesus. For if you are a Green, it means you have only just begun this journey of being conformed into the image of Jesus Christ — and it's a journey that has no end.

Here's to exploring the endless frontiers of God's growth potential.

day eight

AN OLD-FASHIONED ETIQUETTE

My house is governed by a set of rules. And my children know these rules well. No spitting, no yelling, no hitting, no running through the house, no meandering around naked, no complaining, no leaving toys strewn about, and no fussing. Now these are only a few of the Ludy household's governing by-laws, all of which have been implemented with the singular desire to create an atmosphere in which peace, joy, love, sweet conversation, strong friendship, deep intimacy, and a wellspring of kindness might be cultivated.

The Ludy kiddos don't think of these rules as oppressive. And that's because they're not. They are merely the loving dictates of two parents who know that for an honorable atmosphere to be cultivated, Godly virtues must be sponsored, and selfish behaviors must be stamped out. In other words, the rules are our friends.

Now rules, in and of themselves, are not very exciting.

In fact, spend much time focusing on rules and a bad case of indigestion sets in. But rules are necessary for any environment to protect its core values and to promote its purpose for existence. For instance, a fancy restaurant doesn't exist to have rules. It exists to prepare delectable food in a stunning atmosphere and serve it in an elegant fashion. However, a fancy restaurant has rules that help preserve their purpose.

For your entertainment, here are some fancy restaurant rules for the Gable Sands Fish Eatery (a restaurant I made up):

> *At the Gable Sands Fish Eatery, we only utilize fish caught this very day in the Bay of Bengal; we throw out all bread that is dated past fifteen hours old; and we only hire wait-staff that have passed, with flying colors, the Dale Carnegie speaking course.*

These are rules, but they are not oppressive rules. They are not rules employed to make their customers miserable. But, rather, these rules are implemented in order to ensure their customer's satisfaction.

Every well-trained lover has rules. However, since a well-trained lover is most likely of the poetic sort, he doesn't call his rules rules, but his etiquette. And his etiquette is based on one very simple concept: respect. He builds his etiquette around the grand idea of being married to one person for a lifetime. He thinks of "that someday spouse" in all that he does. And he also thinks about everyone else's "someday spouse." And he determines never to step on the toes of the beauty of either his future love story or, for that matter, anyone else's.

As our relationship was developing, Leslie and I had

our rules, or should I say, our etiquette.

- *We were very watchful in our words spoken. Words that would progress the relationship too quickly were monitored carefully. Sacred phrases such as "I love you" were saved and kept significant.*

- *Physical touch was sparingly used, and then, when implemented, it was used only as a means of courtesy.*

- *Aloneness was avoided, unless there was public accountability (i.e. the zoo, a coffee shop, etc.).*

- *I wouldn't progress in my pursuits of Leslie without first gaining blessing from her parents.*

- *Our motto toward all the "gray territory" was "err on the side of caution and not on the side of presumption."*

Yes, I realize that at the outset such notions may sound unromantic and oppressive. But this etiquette wasn't oppressive or unromantic at all. Rather, it was merely the loving dictates of two young romantics who desired an honorable, noble, and God-pleasing relationship to be fostered. And I can personally testify that the romance that flowed out of this etiquette was beautiful beyond description.

Here's to laying down a few good old-fashioned rules.

day nine

HONOR

If you came to me and said, "Eric, I'm headed to Home Depot to pick up a few things to really make my future love story romantic. Any suggestions as to what I should grab while I'm there?"

Well, word to the wise, Home Depot wouldn't be the spot to find it, but if I were to play along with this interesting metaphorical idea, there would be a few necessities that every old-fashioned romantic needs in his tool box. So, here's my shopping list for you.

First, you should look into picking up a keen sense of timing — it's one of those gizmos in the hardware section that helps discern that precise moment for the words to be spoken, or the song to play, or even the proposal made. It's a great little tool to have around.

Second, I would highly encourage you to grab a tube full of poetic flare. It's near the paint department on aisle six, and it's not that big, so you can fit a lot of it into your cart. Poetic flare is a little thingamajig that enables you to say it and say it well. When combined with the keen sense of timing, it really can make a love story sparkle. It turns an everyday Joe into an everyday Shakespeare. It makes love notes sing and whispered sweet nothings truly shine. If you pick up enough of these two items and make sure you never run out, then things like strategically-laid love notes, clandestinely-placed chocolate candies, and "Oh-what-is-this-behind-my-back" bouquets of flowers will never be in short supply.

And thirdly, make sure you pick up all the honor in the store. In fact, go to every store in the state and grab their entire inventory. Honor is essential.

Now that I think about it, go ahead and grab a second cart in order to make sure you purloin all the honor you can get your hands on.

Honor is the tool of tools for the old-fashioned romantic.

Remember how we mentioned etiquette and how significant it is. Well, all the etiquette in the world means nothing if you don't have honor. For, whereas a well-groomed etiquette helps properly direct behavior in challenging and potentially tempting moments and thusly places a guard around purity, honor is what motivates you to keep your etiquette.

After all, when the moment arrives and the opportunity for compromise is at hand, a few rules left in your desk drawer back home have little power of persuasion. In such a moment, you need something more than noble sentiment inside you to be able to truly implement the grand ideas that this book is espousing.

Honor is a God concept. Actually, to be quite specific, it's God's behavior in and through a man or a woman. And to be even more specific, it's God actually living within a man, behaving as only God can behave, wielding the life of a man as His chosen instrument.

Sorry to break it to you, but you can't pick up honor on the shelves of Home Depot.

It's something that only God has on His shelves.

Only God can behave as God.

Only God can always demonstrate the selfless pattern of living. Only God can exhibit the graces of love, truth, and heavenly nobility.

In a sense, God has an etiquette. And God never violates His heavenly etiquette. Never. But that is because He is first and foremost Love. He always does that which is most beneficial to those around Him. He is always seeking the best for others, even if it means His own wallet is taxed.

Think about the Cross.

That was for our benefit, and it wasn't just His heavenly wallet that was taxed. He gave up everything for us.

His etiquette stems from the great Love that He is. He values others, considers others, remembers others, and truly loves others.

And that love-in-action is honor. Honor is love made practical. It's love made specific. It's showing value to the weak by actually giving up your meal to make certain they get a meal. It's opening a door for a lady to demonstrate her high value and your desire to serve. It's graciously leaving a room when you and a member of the opposite sex are the only two in it, as a means of protecting the integrity of the other's reputation. And it's a thousand things like it.

Remember, honor is a God concept. It is God's behavior in and through a man or woman.

So, how does one get this God behavior? You ask.

Well, that's simple.

God's great design isn't to just forgive you for your

past faults, but to overtake your body and make it His very home. And if you are willing, He will make this home (known as you) into a brilliant picture of His grand nobility.

There are a lot of great gizmos and thingamajigs that you can pick up over the years to spruce up your love story, add texture, and greater beauty. But you must have honor as your essential tool.

Here's to asking for big things from a God who delights to do exceedingly abundantly beyond all we could ask or think.

day ten

THE CODE OF WALLACE

Etiquette truly is an exciting and beautiful concept. Every great old-fashioned love story has an etiquette where there is a decided way that a man should treat a lady, a decided way that a lady should treat a man, and a decided way that a noble courtship proceeds. However, there is something even stronger, more dignified, and more enchanting than a well-groomed etiquette that you, as a budding lover, can implement.

It's called a code of honor.

Even the sound of it stirs me. I love the idea of a code of honor. It makes me think of knights and fair maidens — harrowing rescue plots, daring exploits, and gentlemanly decorum.

You see, an etiquette is like a dictionary — defining all terms in detail and with precision — while a code of honor is more like an epic purpose statement with a background movie score underlying it.

A code of honor is born when an everyday man or

woman decides that "everyday" is no longer the order of their life, but that extraordinary living is the new order of things. That is when the background movie score begins to play.

A code of honor is written by the sheer drive of the human soul to see heaven come to earth in and through a human life lived.

A code of honor answers the most profound questions introduced to us by the Cross work of Jesus Christ. For instance...

What would a human life be like if it was indwelled by the Almighty? When such a life would speak, what would it say? When such a life would go from here to there, how would it walk? How would it dress? How would it spend its time?

Great men and women have great codes by which they live. And these codes are grand sweeping reminders of what this Life is all about.

For instance, William Wallace, the great preserver of Scottish liberty, was a man with a code. His code was manly, marvelous, and majestic. It was bigger than any mere man could carry out — it was God-sized.

Nowadays, we make our plans and chart our course based on human ability and not on God's ability. But the old-fashioned way of thinking is that God intends to be God in and through those that simply let Him.

William Wallace lived a grand life, he planned grand adventures, and he accomplished grand things.

How?

He expected his all-powerful God to live all-powerfully in and through him. I love his famous line...

God armeth the patriot!

William Wallace was a true noble heart. He was a man of honor. He was strong when he needed to be strong, and soft in the very moments when softness was required. He was gentle with the ladies and the children, but he was a fierce lion's roar unto those that miscarried justice.

Listen to seven select strains of Wallace's code. Don't forget to underlay it with your favorite background movie score...

- I must never hesitate on the field of battle, even for a moment, to embrace the point of the sword — for honor demands the instant obedience of a soldier.

- I must prove courageous, unmoved by obstacle, undeterred by seeming defeat, dauntless and bravehearted though all have fled and I must stand all alone against ten thousand.

- I must be a workman approved for battle. My hands must be trained for war, my soul trained for endurance in battle. I must be prepared for all manner of warfare, for there is no greater disgrace than a soldier who flees in the midst of the fight.

- I will never attack an unarmed man. I must fight my battles with the same decorum with which God fights His.

- I must never speak ill, even if it be true, of one whose honor I have covenanted to keep. I must never endanger or degrade the ones I love in order to preserve my own life and/or reputation.

- I must prove single-minded in my priority and undeterred by the charms of society — harnessed in my soul, unavailable to the enticements of the flesh, wholly closed off to the invitation of compromise, clear-minded and strong of presence at all times.

- I must hold my conscience sacred. Every word spoken must be weighed before the bar of heaven; every action lived must demonstrate the divine pattern of love, courage, and faith; and every motive of my soul must be measured against the selfless sacrifice of Calvary. My word is my bond, my unbreakable covenant.

THE GREAT ROMANTIC PLAYBOOK

Call me old-fashioned, but I believe what the Bible says. And I don't just believe some of it — I believe all of it. And, though it was written with human penmanship, it is not the words of mere men, but in truth it is the Word of God.

Many postmodernists mock the notion that I just presented in the previous paragraph. They believe that Truth is evolving, ever-changing with the times. But, Truth itself declares that it does not change — ever! For Truth is not a philosophy, a thought, an idea, or a doctrine. It's a Person — a Person who is the same yesterday, today, and forever.

While the postmodern immoralists wax eloquent and philosophical about their "sexual freedoms" and their "personal divinity," I would declare that with all their fancy philosophical notions, these free-livers are morally bankrupt, their marriages stink, their families are falling apart, and they are wholly without a compass. For without the truth (and by truth I mean God's version of it), a man is without a foundation, without a north by which to calibrate his compass, and without a hope in the world.

Either the Bible is true or it's not. If it's true, then heed what it says with grand gusto. If it's not, then don't waste your time.

My old-fashioned ideals are better classified as ancient ideals, because they have been around since the beginning. They are not my own ideas. They are God's ideas. And where do you think I found them? Uh-huh...in the Bible.

Just think about it...

God is the One who made man and woman. He is the One that intended them for each other. He is the One that set boundaries of appropriate interaction between the sexes. He is the One that invented marriage. He came up with the idea of sex. He is Love. His behavior is Perfect Love. He is the model Bridegroom. He laid down His life for His Bride and says, "This is how love works — this is what it looks like!" He designed marriage to be 'till death parts — it's called covenant. He set the standard of measurement and said, "Now this is excellence! This pleases Me!"

The God of the Universe has spoken, but most of us have ignored Him. We've shrugged our shoulders and declared that we prefer our own philosophies and moral viewpoints over His. After all, His ideas are so old-fashioned.

But, let me point out that His ideas are the only ones that actually work.

For instance, use my life as a test case.

To me, the Bible has authority to tell me what to

do — it's my commander, my king, my general.

Am I miserable because of it?

No. In fact, I'm convinced I'm the happiest man on planet earth today. I've wished for some time that there was an Olympic event for sheer happiness — because I think I would take the gold medal.

Even at the risk of sounding massively biased, I think I have the greatest love story EVER. And, as logically follows, I have arguably the most amazing marriage around and the most exquisite and enchanting wife. I have six of the happiest, giggly kiddos. I love my life, and not because it's easy (it's actually stacked with trials), but because God has built my life to perfectly match what I am wired to be doing. I am able to laugh in difficulty, leap for joy in crisis, and sing in the darkest hour. I wouldn't trade my life for anyone else's on planet Earth — and I really mean that.

And all this simply because I chose to say, "God knows best."

For those of you who have been giving the questioning eye toward the Bible your entire life, my encouragement to you today is that, instead, you begin to direct your questioning eye towards your personal belief system that has been constructed out of your own head.

God is right. His ways are right. And it shouldn't come as any surprise, but His ways actually work. Yes, they may seem a bit old-fashioned. But maybe that shouldn't be deemed bad. After all, it's not as if our newly-fashioned notions are supplying a lot of happily-ever-after these days.

Here's to picking up the Bible, the ultimate authoritative guide for romantic lovers, and letting it once again direct our love stories.

day twelve

INVESTING THE PENNY

Maybe it's obvious that great love stories need lots of love, but there is another very sizable and significant ingredient that is not as obvious to the casual observer of great and lasting romance. And this oft-forgotten ingredient is an absolute must for a love story to thrive and never die.

Faith.

Yes, I realize that the word faith sounds like something that belongs in a church building and not something that belongs in a love story. But without it the whole love system shuts down, because everything in the entire love operation operates with it.

For instance. If you want grace, the Bible makes it clear that you need faith. If you want to know God's love and live in God's love, again, it's faith that supplies the ticket. Moral excellence? Yep, faith. Honor? Uh-huh, faith. Set-apartness? Faith. Faithfulness 'till death do us part? Faith.

Everything that makes love sparkle is gained by faith. And every love story that could ever please God is built out of the stuff. It says in Hebrews 11:6 that "without faith it is impossible to please Him." Then again in Galatians 5:6, "the only thing that counts is faith expressing itself in love" (NIV). Oh, and yet again in Ephesians 2:8, "For by grace you have been saved through faith." It would appear that a lot rests on this idea of "faith," and in fact, a lot does — and not just in life and eternal matters, but in love.

So, what exactly is faith? And how does one access the stuff? Or if you already have a little of it, how does one go about getting more?

Technically, such a question deserves a bit more than just a few lines in a book to be properly answered. But I will give you my abbreviated answer and hopefully it will be enough to get you aimed in the right direction.

Faith is simply believing that when God says something is true, it's true. It's a decision of the soul to agree with God, to trust that He knows what He is doing.

So, when it comes to romance, faith is trusting that what God says about it is true, and it's deciding to agree with God instead of arguing with Him over the point. It's declaring, with your very lifestyle, that God knows what He is doing. And it's changing your life around to fit with God's take on reality. In other words, real faith truly alters a life.

This means that if you are measuring in the Red Zone, you must switch around your way of doing things and instead of trusting yourself to be right, you must start trusting that God is right. And thusly, you must stop all forward progress in your current relationship and focus on first things first — and that is getting your relationship right with God.

Hebrews 11:6 says, "...he who comes to God must believe that He is, and that He is a rewarder of those who diligently seek Him."

We must trust that God is real — in other words, He IS. But not just that He is there, but that if someone diligently seeks Him and goes after His way they will be personally rewarded by Him, the God of the Universe.

Romance is an issue that demands trust. It takes faith to walk away from an unhealthy relationship and declare, "God will take care of me." It takes faith to pause a relationship, wait, watch, and pray — declaring, "God will grant me grace in the waiting." And, it takes faith to progress a relationship on God's terms, in God's manner, in God's timing, with God's honor governing the entire process — declaring, "God will lead us every step of the way."

You may only have a penny of faith as you are reading this. Your amount of confidence in God might only be a penny's worth. But if you have a penny — a penny's a penny. And I encourage you to invest that little penny of faith this very day in the Person of God. He will not fail you. Trust Him and you will not be put to shame.

Here's to leaning our weight and our confidence on the only One who can truly hold us up.

day thirteen

THE BODY

To properly understand sexuality, you must understand the human body. And I don't just mean the biology of the human body — but the way the whole operation works (outside and inside). Because if you don't understand how the body works, then certain factions within your body will run the show and attempt to seize control of the formation of your love story. But, if you do understand the different factions and power struggles within your body, then your body can be put in its proper place and actually become a useful tool in this whole romantic schematic.

So, over the next three days, we are going to explore this strange, bizarre, super-intriguing, and tremendously important concept of the human body.

The first thing we need to address is the big picture.

You are stuck in a body. You didn't have any choice in the matter, and now, for better or for worse, you are wearing this particular body suit and there is no getting out of it and no swapping it out.

And, have you noticed that our bodies supply us complications in this life? For instance, our bodies need to eat. They need to sleep. They have cravings, urges, longings, hungerings, thirstings, and every other sort of inconvenient desire. And, let's face it — our lives would go a lot smoother if we didn't have to care for these bodies. And relating to the opposite sex would be an entirely different proposition if it didn't involve human bodies.

Now, don't get me wrong. I'm not proposing that the human body is bad; it's just that if its role is not properly understood, then things get out of control in no time.

So, let's figure this whole human body thing out.

Let's start by noting that you and your body both have the same name. I'm called Eric Ludy, and, when people point at my body, they say, "There goes Eric Ludy." However, me and my body are different. I'm me, and well, my body is, uh, my body.

For the sake of clear titles, let's refer to me as "Self," while we can refer to my body with the novel title of "Body."

Imagine the life of Eric Ludy as if it was a factory operation known as "Eric Ludy's Fancy Fruits, Inc." In this scenario, my personal Body would be the warehouse in which all the factory machines did their sputtering, cranking, and producing. But Self would be the guy in the back room that sits in the director's chair responsible for the operation.

The Bible makes it clear that the human body was created to produce a very specific sort of fruit (i.e. love, joy, peace, patience, kindness, goodness, faith, gentleness, and self-control). Our machines are supposed to be producing this supernatural good and tasty fruit, but something is wrong with our operation, and all of the fruit coming out of our machines is off — it stinks, it's rotten, and it can't please God.

The Bible also makes it clear that the reason we are producing such bad fruit is due to the fact that we have a terrible problem inside of us.

It appears that Self was never supposed to claim the glassed-in office as his own. He wasn't supposed to sit down in that director's chair. And everything went wrong when he did.

According to the Bible, that glassed-in office belongs to Jesus Christ and that chair is His chair. He bought this factory with His very life's blood and, in order for this factory to function as it ought, the glassed-in office needs to become His office, and the director's chair, His chair.

When Self sits in the control position of the human body, the Bible calls it Sin. It's Self claiming a rank and a preeminence that it was never supposed to claim within the Body.

Since the word "sin" is such a religious sounding word, a more pedestrian term for this undue Self-promotion is Selfishness. And this Selfishness is the root of every problem in this world. It is the root of every sexual disorder, every broken heart, every divorce, every harsh word, every cheating excursion, and every flirtatious escapade.

We all have a body, we all have a glassed-in office, and we all have a director's chair. But the key question is, "Who is currently sitting on the director's chair in our life?"

If it is you, then it is time to step down.

Whoever sits in that chair in your Body is the one responsible for the fruit born.

If it is you, you will not be able to produce the fruit necessary to walk in the abundance of great love and intimacy.

But, if it is Jesus, then you will find that good fruit just comes bursting forth as a matter of course. For where He is present, love, joy, peace, patience, kindness, goodness, faith, gentleness, and self-control are right there with Him in ever-increasing measure.

Great love stories can't help but become great when the Author of Love and Romance moves into His rightful place.

Here's to bearing some truly fancy heavenly fruit.

THE ALL-IMPORTANT THRONE

The human body is very interesting place, full of intrigue, power struggles, and coupe attempts. It's a bit like the government of Somalia. And most of us would admit that Somalia isn't the place most consider ideal for honeymooning.

And this is why it is critical that our bodies become a place fit for a honeymoon getaway — marked by peace, order, love, life, beauty, and nice sandy beaches.

So, as a quick review:

You have a body, but you are not your body, you are you — a.k.a. Self.

Inside your body, there is a control deck, a captain's quarters, a glassed-in office. And depending on who sits in that office — in the nice leather high-backed chair (historically known as The Throne) — the body will either produce good fruit or bad fruit.

And, just to be clear: it's not supposed to be you sitting in that control position of your life.

Your derriere + nice leather high-backed chair = bad fruit.

But Jesus in that chair equals good fruit.

I don't know if you've noticed, but we all have a strange itch, a bizarre attraction for that director's chair. And there isn't a single one of us that hasn't sat down in that nice, soft leather and sinned.

You see, the problem with us sitting in that director's chair isn't merely the rebellion, the self-aggrandizement, and the general idiocy of the maneuver — it's the ever-binding effects of doing it.

We don't realize it, but to sit in that chair is to legally decline the grace of God and turn ourselves over to a dark power. It might feel like a thrill to take the helm of the human life and claim, "Mine!" But, in doing so, we are sticking our head under the boot of the Enemy.

I've introduced you to two very key characters thus far — Self and the Body. But there is an ugly, disgusting third character that I loath to mention, but have no alternative.

His name is Flesh.

In the Bible he is referred to with different names. For instance, he is the principle of sin, the sin nature, the old man, and even the law of sin and death. But trust me when I say it doesn't matter which name he's wearing — he's bad news.

The best way to describe Flesh is to think of a rabid dog, foaming at the mouth. He's irrational, dangerous, self-serving, and quite disturbing. Well, then imagine sticking that same rabid dog, in his unstable state, in charge of your Body.

You see, Self was designed by God to serve. And thusly, Self will serve something. If Jesus sits in His proper seat in the human body, then Self is free to serve Him — free to walk in the dignity of royal manner; free to be pure, loving, noble, holy, kind, gentle, courageous, and every other virtue. However, if Self usurps an unlawful position in the Body and sits where he is not supposed to sit, then, legally, the frothing dog takes control, and we are no longer free to serve Christ and to do that which is good and pleasing, but are now subservient only to that which is selfish, debased, destructive, and disgusting.

If you have ever wondered why someone can esteem love, purity, nobility, courage, and kindness but be wholly unable to live them out, this is the reason.

Many of us sit on the throne of our life, desiring to make our lives succeed, thirsting for real virtue, hungering for a true godly love story, but the desire itself is not enough to wrench us from sin. For once you sit down in that chair, you are legally bound. You are stuck, and you are stuck forever — for eternity enjoined to the wages of such a decision.

There is only One who can get you out of that seat. There is only One that can remove Flesh, the rabid dog from the control position over your body. There is only One that can set your Body in working order, the way it was originally intended to be.

Please, I implore you. Allow Jesus His rightful place.

When you call on Jesus, He will swiftly remove Flesh from the premises and He will untie the rope that binds you to that director's chair. And He will kindly say to you, "Please, step down."

If you step down, Flesh will have no legal access to come back in.

But, if you refuse Christ's kind offer of rescue and

do not step down from your unlawful control position in your Body, then, though you called upon Jesus, the benefits of His rescue will be lost upon you. For legally, as long as you sit in that chair, Flesh will rule your life and the fruit you bear will stink to the high heavens.

So, if you are looking for a love story without foam around its mouth, then I would highly encourage you to let Jesus do His work and get you off that throne.

Here's to stepping down so that our rightful King can ascend to His proper seat.

day fifteen

THE GOOD NEWS

Do you remember Flesh, the rabid dog I introduced you to yesterday? To jog your memory, he was the irrational, dangerous, self-serving, and disturbing character who is hell-bent on controlling your body and ruining your life. Remember, he is the one who only has control when you, Self, sit in the director's chair in your body.

Well, Flesh loves pleasure. And as a result, we often find ourselves actually missing his antics when he is removed from the premises of our life. Because, to be quite honest, we love pleasure too.

Flesh is sort of like a bad smoking habit finally broken, that every-so-often skulks about outside the windows of our lives pleading, "Come on, man, just one draw, just one puff for old time's sake."

Flesh is sort of like Donny Lucero, the guy with a locker right next to mine during my high school days. Donny was an irrational, dangerous, self-serving, and disturbing character who only had one thing on his mind. Part of me wanted to stay far and away from him. But he was a self-proclaimed Doctor of Pleasure, and, as a result, I often found myself tantalized by his tales, intrigued by his lifestyle, and secretly desirous of sharing in his plunder.

Donny treated girls with contempt. He robbed their purity and left them with nothing but cool nonchalance in return. Everything Donny did was disgusting, rude, and debased. He was selfish — and he was only nice, courteous, and complimentary to con a girl into giving her purity to him.

It's not just me that grew up with a locker next to Donny. In a sense, we all did. We all had his chortled voice speaking to us throughout the day, beckoning us to compromise and choose the depraved way.

But if you desire romance the way God intended it, in all its beauty and grandeur, you must make a decisive statement on the matter of Donny's behavior once and for all. Either you stand with Donny and his disgusting antics, or you side against Donny and accept his mockery and slights. To choose respect, honor, dignity, and nobility means to pointedly state to Donny, "You are disgusting and I don't want to have anything to do with you — ever again."

The human body was built by God to serve others and to please God. God made it "very good." But we have an enemy who wants, more than anything, to sabotage how our bodies work. This is where the Serpent and forbidden fruit comes into the picture. For when we heed God's ways, life works. But when we doubt God's ways and side with the Serpent and his rebellious enticements, lo and behold, we find our Self seated in an unlawful position on a throne that is not ours to sit on — and we find a disgusting, drooling, debased Donny ruling the roost within our body.

Just to review. Jesus has supplied an opportunity to

each one of us. It's an escape from our unlawful rebellious position seated on that Throne in the director's office. We've been offered the freedom to finally step down, and thusly see the perverted Flesh lose its power over our bodies.

It's an amazing fact. But the Flesh no longer can control your life — or your love story — if you allow Jesus Christ to rescue you from your Self. It's called Good News.

But just because the Flesh loses its power at the Cross, it's important to note his cunning, duplicitous behavior, in order that he doesn't sneak back in and take charge over your body once again.

The Flesh is sort of like the law of gravity. It's just there, and it has always been there. And, like the law of gravity, it has power over you, to keep you in the dirt as long as you live a normal, everyday, Self-on-the-throne life. But, amazingly, there is a law higher than gravity that exists — it's called the law of aerodynamics. And so, if you hop on board an airplane, the law of gravity is powerless over you. It is trumped by a higher law. So, as long as you remain in the airplane, there is a victory, a strength, a power, and a virtue that is supplied to you in order to live in a new way — a way that was previously impossible to you. It's called flight.

But, just outside that airplane (which, by the way, in this illustration is Jesus Christ), the law of gravity still very much exists. If gravity knocked on the window of the plane and shouted, "Hey, you in there! You don't need to always stay in the airplane! That's old-fashioned, repressive, legalistic, puritanical, boringness! Come out here and breathe the open air of freedom for a minute — you will see what you are missing!"

Why would we open the door?

Most of us fall for the Flesh's bait. We don't want to be "old-fashioned, repressive, legalistic, puritanical bores." So we throw open the door every now and again just to free ourselves from such a stigma. But what we find the moment we open the door to the plane is that the law of gravity still has power as long as we submit to it. Likewise, the Flesh is not dead (as in vanished, buried, no more a threat); it's that we are dead to the Flesh's power as long as we remain firmly planted in Jesus Christ.

It might sound a bit old-fashioned to say it, but I encourage you to listen closely and do your best to not cringe at how outdated this advice might sound, but, please don't ever listen to the bait of the Flesh. Do not heed his advice. Do not follow his bread trails of temptation. He has absolutely nothing good to offer. His ways lead to destruction, decomposition, divorce, and disaster.

Here's to remaining in the plane...forever, always, and happily ever after.

day sixteen

THE POWER OF GRACE

There is a modern notion floating around out there called humanitarianism. For all practical purposes, it's a good sounding notion. It's about helping, it's about giving, it's about serving, and it's about loving. Sounds like a winning idea, doesn't it?

But there is an inherent problem with this idea of humanitarianism. It's a way of helping, giving, serving, and loving that excludes God. It is humankind declaring, "We don't need God's help — we can do this ourselves."

The definition of humanitarianism at dictionary.com is quite telling.

Hu·man·i·tar·i·an·ism:
the doctrine that humankind may become perfect without divine aid.

A lot of us try and take this same doctrine into our love stories. If our modern romance mentality were on dictionary.com, it would probably read something like this:

Mo·dern Ro·mance:
the idea that love stories may become perfect without divine aid.

Remember, this book is about the old-fashioned etiquette of falling in love. So, I wouldn't be doing you any favors if I didn't sound a bit old-fashioned throughout the pages of this book.

I'm going to propose that it's not just that you need God's ideas, His old-fashioned ways, and His honorable formula for success in order to have a great love story. I'm going to go one step further. I'm going to say, you need divine aid in the most personal form. You need Jesus, the Great Author of Romance Himself, to come and live inside you — to love through you, to show kindness through you, to serve through you, and to be the ultimate romantic through you.

This is the age-old concept of covenant exchange. It's what a marriage ceremony is all about. Two lovers exchange rings, vows, kisses, and googly eyes. A marriage is an exchange. The man says to the woman, "All I have and all I am, I give to you." And then the woman says to the man, "And all I have and all I am, I give to you." It's an exchange of love, life, possessions, protection, body, intimacy, and trust. It's all you have and are for all they have and are.

But this marriage ceremony is merely an earthly picture of the covenant exchange God ask us to make with Him.

At the Cross, He said, "All I have and all I am, I give to you." And He meant it. It was His vow, His seal of covenant, His kiss (as it were), and His affectionate invitation for us to return the vow.

This is the centerpiece of marriage intimacy. Without

covenant exchange God doesn't have access to you, and without covenant exchange you don't have access to God.

So, to make it quite simple: God is asking for your body. He is asking for your life. He is asking for your future. And He is also asking for your love story.

But remember: this is an exchange. He asks for everything from you, and you now have access to everything from Him. And He possesses everything you need to succeed in this life. Everything you will ever need for life and godliness is stored away in the Person of Jesus Christ. Everything you could ever need to love one person for a lifetime — you have in Him. Everything you will ever need for kindness, gentleness, courage, boldness, purity, integrity, and faithfulness is found in Him.

By the way, when the Bible uses the word grace, this is what it is talking about. It's God at work in the human body — revealing His grand and glorious behavior in and through a life wholly yielded to Him. Grace is not just a merciful idea; it's an empowered idea. It lifts weak humanity up out of the mud, washes it clean, sets it solidly upon a rock, and then causes it to triumph.

That's biblical grace.

So, let's look at the definition of a romance built God's way as it might appear on dictionary.com:

Old·Fash·ion·ed·Ro·mance:
the idea that without divine aid there is no hope of a love story ever turning out perfect, but that with divine aid, it can't help but become a picture of heaven-on-earth.

Here's to asking God for a little more grace.

day seventeen

THE POWER OF FORGIVENESS

Unforgiveness is something that will cripple a marriage. And not just the marriage, but it will cripple all those who drink of its poison.

A relationship that thrives must know the old-fashioned art of forgiving and being forgivable.

Forgiveness is like a door into a vault where all the gold is stored. If forgiveness is not offered to the perpetrator and a grievance is carried, then the door is left ajar. Unforgiveness is like a bleeping neon sign to all the powers of hell, shouting, "Free gold for the taking — this idiot left the door open!" Your vault will be plundered within twenty-four hours guaranteed.

And unforgiveness doesn't just give away the virtue of your vault; it also invites darkness to come in and takes its place. Every time they take a bar of gold, they replace it with a bar of bitterness and resentment. And pretty soon, there is a disease inside your soul — a dark, heavy pressure upon your heart, a gloomy, dull, lifeless yuck plunked down like a massive sack of rancid potatoes in your being.

There are two kinds of forgiveness.

Human forgiveness
God forgiveness

Human forgiveness is a good thing. After all, it closes the door to the vault and lets the offender off the hook within your soul. But, human forgiveness has its limitations. It leaves you with a blankness, a coolness, and a chill towards the person that you forgave. You may not hold anything bad against them, but you also don't hold anything good toward them. They aren't your enemy, but they also aren't your friend.

Human forgiveness stops the minions of darkness from stealing your gold bars of virtue, and it does keep the bitterness and resentment from entering into your vault — but it doesn't truly do all that God intended forgiveness to do.

Human forgiveness is what Dr. Phil will teach you. But good, old-fashioned God forgiveness is what I want to teach you.

When God forgives, He doesn't just go blank and cool towards those He forgives. Instead, He turns into their greatest champion — He blesses them, He invites them near, and He gives His very best. It seems wholly crazy when you first see it. But this is the basis of the work on the Cross.

If you want to be great in love and relationships, this is a must. You must learn to forgive the way God forgives. And to do that, you will need God to do this in and through you (for it's more than we can pull off on our own).

In the Bible, Jesus tells a story about a king who is collecting his debts and he comes across one of his servants who owes an extraordinary, suffocating, and un-payable amount. The servant begs the king to show him mercy and to allow him more time to pay it. The king does more than that. He completely forgives the debt. Wow! But here is where the story takes a turn. The newly forgiven servant goes out and finds someone who owes him a very small amount of money and demands it of him immediately. This indebted man begs the king's servant for leniency and grace, but the servant offers him none, and instead throws him into debtor's prison until he can pay every last cent. When the king hears word of this travesty, he throws the once-forgiven servant into prison and demands him to pay back every cent.

Yes, it's a rather depressing story, I admit. But it has an amazing truth stored within it.

If we have been forgiven our massive debt by God, how can we possibly justify not forgiving others the small, trifling debts they have outstanding towards us?

This is the basis of a non-stop success story in marriage.

When you mess up, be forgivable — go seek forgiveness and quickly.

When your spouse messes up and hurts you, be forgiving — instantly forgive, with the God-variety of forgiveness, and then become their greatest champion and bless them until their socks come off.

If you want to be prepared to live, love, and forgive well, then you need to start now. If there is anyone in your life that needs to be forgiven, please ask God to help you do this right, even today. Get clean of this gunk. And when you forgive, don't just go through the motions of human forgiveness, but allow God to forgive them, love them, and bless them through you.

They may not deserve your forgiveness, but remember: neither did you deserve the forgiveness you received from the Cross.

Here's to seeing the golden virtue brought back into the vault.

GETTING RID OF THE BAGGAGE

When I was twenty-eight years old, I found myself in a hospital bed with extreme chest pains, shortness of breath, and a very big problem.

You see, I was addicted to stress and I was controlled by anxiety.

That was thirteen years ago, and I am a completely different man today. Today I'm so happy I feel like I'm going to burst and, though my life is one hundred times more challenging than it was thirteen years ago, I have zero anxiety.

Obviously something changed inside of me. And it is important that what changed inside of me changes inside of you. For there is nothing more unromantic than a hospital bed, extreme chest pains, and shortness of breath — except for maybe a catheter, a bed pan, and one of those hospital gowns.

It all started around our first anniversary when I was packing up all our belongings to move back to Colorado from Michigan. The whole packing process was intense, supremely stressful, and disorderly. So, when I finally closed the lock on the back of the Ryder truck, I let out a woeful sigh and limped back into our condominium.

That is when I saw it. Our backyard grill was still sitting there like a mocking ugly troll upon our back deck.

It was at that moment that Anxiety came to the door of my soul and begged for entry. He reasoned with me that he was deserving of entry, that it was only reasonable I would permit him entry, and that, if he came in, he could somehow make me feel better than I was feeling at that precise moment.

As a believer in Jesus, I hadn't ever really dealt with Anxiety up to that point in time. But something about Anxiety's argument convinced me. And in that moment, I legally allowed him access into my life.

I ended up on the floor of our condominium, paralyzed, lying there like a defeated foe.

Then, for the next four years of my life, this crazy varmint, Anxiety, continued to be my companion. He was crushing me — weighing down upon my chest like a thousand-pound barbell. I didn't want him around, but I couldn't get him away. And there I was lying in a hospital bed hooked up to an EKG four years later.

What I didn't realize was how the legalities of sin work. Anxiety had legal right to be there due to my ignorant and idiotic behavior four years prior. I allowed him entrance and had never corrected my mistake.

When you know Jesus Christ, these things are not allowed to linger in your life.

For me it was anxiety. But there are plenty of things like it that many of us are currently lugging around. I think the operative word is "baggage." And this baggage will do our future marriage not a single bit of good. So, let's get rid of it.

For some it's fear. We invited it in and have shown hospitality to it, and now in every situation we hear its voice, heed its council, and live a coward's life.

For some it's lust. We invited it in and now it has completely warped our perception of love, intimacy, and purity. We can't seem to see sex as something either good or pure, let alone godly. Though we may live a respectable life outwardly, inside we are perverted, moral felons and disgusting even to ourselves.

For some it's pride. We can't seem to imagine a life that doesn't center around us, our opinions, our feelings, and our tastes. We don't just sit on the throne of our lives, but we have elaborate justifications for why we are the best ones suited to sit there.

Of course, there are many other things we could name. But they are all built out of the same wicked stuff. And that is our legal authorization.

The way Jesus works is quite simple.

He sticks His finger on these things and shows us that these things must go. He shows us the Cross and demonstrates to us that these operations of darkness have no legal right to stay around. And then He tells us to tell them to go, to leave, to vamoose. But He says, "Make sure you tell them to go 'in My Name.' For they only fear Me and they MUST heed Me."

A great love story isn't constantly burdened by the baggage of sin. Anxiety, fear, lust, and pride do not rule the relationship — God does.

So, let your body know — and let the enemy and his

camp know — that you mean business. Let them know that you are no longer going to be a pushover and a plaything for them, but are going to begin to live in accordance with Jesus Christ — His rules, His way.

Here's to a future honeymoon without all that baggage to lug along.

day nineteen

MADE NEW

Hebrews 12:1 says, "...let us lay aside every weight, and the sin which doth so easily beset us, and let us run with patience the race that is set before us."

As we discussed yesterday, there is an old, disgusting life that we are needing to throw off, cast away, and, as Hebrews 12:1 says, "lay aside." We have old patterns, old thoughts, old mentalities, old journals, old love notes, old trophies, and old memories that are twisted and wrong. They need to find their way to the trash.

With every death of the old comes a birth of the new. And every converted lover must have a new beginning.

My new beginning was on February 2, 1990. I remember writing in my journal that day, "New Beginning." It was my fresh start. Old things were passed away, behold, all things were become new. I was a new person. Yes, I still bore the same name. I still had the same curly black hair. But I was new.

But just because I was new didn't mean I was a finished work. And twenty-two years later, I'm still not finished. It's called the process of maturity.

Twenty-two years ago I was made new, but I wasn't

made finished. I had to be retrained, rebuilt, reformatted. My mind had a lot of junk in it that had to be overwritten. My eyes were used to perusing women and selfishly taking what I observed for myself and my own gratification — and this had to change. My mouth was used to speaking things that were not profitable to anyone or anything — and suddenly I realized that my speech needed to change.

My whole life was changed.

I used to wake up in the morning and shower, dress, primp, and spritz the cologne on for one singular purpose: to be noticed. Suddenly, I had a higher purpose, a nobler purpose for living.

I used to prowl about for girls. Now I found myself learning to protect them from those guys who were on the prowl.

I used to flirt with girls. Now I found myself not wanting to do anything that might mislead their hearts.

I had become strange, odd, and yes, old-fashioned.

That's just what God does. He makes His men and women to behave as He would behave. And, as a result, we look strange to this world, odd to our peers, and funny to our contemporaries. But, in heaven's eyes, we look completely normal.

We each have old patterns that need to be thrown out. Some of us only have our parents' marriage to look to for an example, and it's simply not healthy. Some of us only have the pattern of Hollywood when it comes to taking steps forward in a romantic relationship. But that pattern doesn't actually work in real life. It is false, duplicitous, lust-driven, and will only set you up for a great failure.

This book won't be able to take you to the heights of noble love. It's just a book. But hopefully this book will be able to introduce you well to the One who can.

Here's to being made new.

(

day twenty

THE OLYMPIC-LEVEL LOVER

Once you catch the vision of a God-built love story, your mind can't help but ask some serious and lofty questions.

If God were to build a love story, is there any limit to how great He might make it?

And if God were to build a lover for a love story how amazing might He actually make them?

Most of us do not see any levels in the notion of romance. There is just one level, one sort of love story, one sort of lover, and we all are on the same level. And the way that we explain the fact that some marriages work and some don't is due to things like "luck," and "chance," and "fortune." But that is preposterous.

You get out of marriage that which you put in to it.

If you invest only a few measly pennies of your life, your energies, and your givenness, then you are only going to get back a smarmish return.

But if you give everything — if you empty your bank account and actually lay it all on the line — then the world cannot contain the beauty, the richness, and the bounty that is certain to come.

There are a lot of great gymnasts. But there are only a handful that make it to the Olympic Games. Why is that?

Well, yes, some of it does have to do with God-given talent. But there is another attribute to an Olympic contender that is important to point out. They are not just talented; they are given to their sport — they are wholly invested in their craft, they have become masters of their talent, and not just carriers of their talent.

The same is true with great romantics. They are Olympic contenders in their focus. They start training for excellence in their future marriage long before they even meet the person they will one day marry. They start loving well — now. They start serving well — now. They start doing thoughtful things — now. They start speaking kindly — now. They start practicing faithfulness unto one — now.

So, if there was an Olympic event entitled "Excellence in Marriage," it would be fascinating to see what might show up from around the world come the big event. I'm not sure how it could possibly be measured (i.e. longest, most passionate kiss seems a bit awkward). But still, it would be amazing to see what would happen if couples actually gave themselves to the pursuit of excellence in an arena that actually matters.

Most of us reading this have not spent our lives up to this point preparing to be excellent in marriage. Thus far, maybe we've only invested pennies into our relationships. But today is the perfect day to empty out our fund and give everything.

Has anyone ever told you it is never too late do things

right? I know, I know — it's one of those old-fashioned sort of quotes, but, you have to admit, it's a good one.

Here's to training to have history's greatest marriage.

day twenty-one

MEN

Men.

Nowadays, they just aren't what they used to be.

Words like gallant, noble, honorable, honest, gentle, kind, and brave need to make a comeback. For men are built to wear such words like noble crowns.

I would liken men to steel hammers. They are built for the most difficult and dangerous tasks.

They are designed to laugh at danger, ridicule ease, smirk at incoming flying bullets, and hold mediocrity in contempt. They take nails, plant their faces courageously on them, and pound them into the wood to hold the infrastructure together. Men fix things. If there is a problem, men are not built to sidle up to it and hug it, but to plug the leak, detangle the tangle, and straighten that which is crooked.

I realize that such a version of manhood is strangely missing in our modern day, but instead of pondering what has happened to such old-fashioned greatness, I would rather talk about what might bring it back to the stage of time in this very generation.

It starts with you.

That's right.

If you are a man, then be a man.

If you are a woman, then catch the vision of noble masculinity and become its biggest champion.

Men are designed by God to be the initiators. Men are the ones who are supposed to take the first steps forward in love and romance. They are the ones who ask the girl to dance. They are the ones who ask the father for the girl's hand. They are the ones who say the words, "Will you marry me?" In other words, men are the risk-takers.

It might seem old-fashioned and socially absurd to consider that men should still do such things. For this is a new day — a day of women's liberation. But even though we, as a society, might be a little more understanding in the realm of a woman's strength, intellect, and potential, this by no means has changed God's ways of doing things. He made the man the initiator, and He hasn't done anything to change that fact. And, just to note, God is not a chauvinist. He's known all along that women were capable. After all, He doesn't make anything subpar. He asks a man to lead because He so greatly treasures femininity.

When God came to this earth, He came as a man. And this was not on accident. He was being the initiator in a great love story. There was a bullet flying through the air, headed straight at the heart of His beloved Bride, and He nobly stepped in front and took the bullet for her.

Jesus even proposed to His Bride while He was here. When a man proposed to his bride in the Hebrew culture, he would set a glass of wine in front her. If she drank, she would be accepting the covenant proposal. The Last Supper was a proposal of covenant. And Christ's Bride accepted.

Jesus chose us; we didn't choose Him. He is the initiator and we are the responders.

I recognize that such notions seem outright bizarre in our modern day. But the beauty and dignity that can be gained by returning to such patterns is incalculable.

The return of true old-fashioned manhood is a challenge for two reasons.

Men have to catch the vision

Women have to allow men to catch the vision

It takes guts for a man to begin to initiate, and it's hard work. It's far easier for a man to let the women lead the show. Let her ask him to dance. Let her plan the dates. Let her pay for the meal. Let her pop the questions. Let her plan the wedding. Let her define the marriage. But, though it be easy, there has never been one woman alive who ever respected her husband when he let her do all these things.

A man in marriage learns his behavior prior to marriage. If the woman leads in the beginning of a relationship, then she continues to lead for the entirety of the relationship. That is, unless something dramatically alters.

Men, I exhort you to rise up and do what you were built to do. And when you do it, do it as a man ought to do it: kindly, courageously, gently, lovingly, honorably, and nobly.

Women, I exhort you to be patient, restrain your natural impulse to take charge, and wait for the man to be the man. If you want a strong man in marriage, then let him start off on the right foot prior to marriage. Strong women, when rightly governed by the grace of God, help make the strongest, most noble men.

Here's to boldly going where no man has gone before.

MEN II

Men.

They are not just males. There is something more to a man than just being biologically male.

A car body is not truly an operative car. It needs the engine to function as it ought. And that is precisely the same with manhood. A male needs the manly engine planted inside his chest to truly begin to operate properly.

And just to clarify, the manly engine is not growling, sweating, hunting, fishing, jumping, ice-climbing, mountaineering, and running with the bulls in Pamplona. Those are things that certain sorts of men enjoy doing, but they aren't necessarily that which defines a man to be manly.

Let's see if we can define the manly engine.

A true man is strong in the very moment when strength is most required. And yet, he is soft in the precise moment when softness is most needed. A true man is manly because he is the perfect hero. He is exactly what is needed in the moment, and yet, without a stitch of compromise.

If he hears the scream for help, a true man is built to

go running into the danger, without care for himself, and rescue the damsel in distress.

And, if he hears the groans of weakness, a true man is designed to reach down and gently pick up the fainting lady, sensitively place her on the back of his white steed, and carry her off to find shelter and sustenance.

That's just good old-fashioned nobility.

A man is groomed to be Jesus in all circumstances. He's a warrior-poet, a weeping prophet, an iron fist in a velvet glove. He's strength, but only to those who pose danger to his precious ones. And he is wholly gentle to the ones he has vowed to protect. He's the growling bear to the wrongdoers, and a soft teddy to the innocent.

Manhood is something that must be practiced. It can't just be esteemed. It must be implemented.

Most of us don't live in the lands of flying bullets and fainting ladies, and therefore we have to take storybook manhood, bring it down to earth, and make it practical.

So, let's practice on a simple date between a man and a woman:

First, the man can offer to drive.

Then, the man can open the car door for the woman and ensure that her hands and feet are in the car prior to shutting the door.

Then, if the car belongs to the woman, the man can offer to stop off at the gas station and fill up the tank.

Then, the man can close the doors and windows to the car while he's putting gas in the tank, so as not to allow the noxious fumes to get into the vehicle.

Then, the man can ask the woman where she would like to eat.

If the woman says McDonalds, then the man should

declare that, for the woman's health and safety, he would prefer a higher quality fare, and then he can make a suggestion.

If the woman still says McDonalds, then so be it, but if she agrees to the man's suggestion, the man can navigate the vehicle up to the entrance and, leaving the car running, put the vehicle in park, hop out of the car, run around to the passenger door, open it, offer his hand, and kindly escort the woman out of the vehicle and safely to the curb, and, depending on her desires, either leave her there or escort her inside the restaurant.

Then, the man can go and find a parking spot, park, and hurriedly make his way to the woman's side once again.

Then, he can go up to the hostess and request a seat for two, and then add any romantic preferences to his request (i.e. outside on the veranda, a spot next to the window, a booth in a private corner, etc.).

The list could go on throughout the night. The man should lead in conversation, ensure the woman's comfort, pay the entirety of the bill, and be responsible for caretaking the entire way. And when strength is required, he shows it (i.e. when the waiter brings out the wrong dish to his date, he personally requests it be made right, and waits patiently to eat his own food until all is set in order). And when softness is needed, he supplies it (i.e. a little child trips on his way through the restaurant and knocks over the man's drink right into his lap — it's an embarrassing mess, but the man, sensitive to the feelings of the little child, is quick to dismiss it and declare it a non-issue, offering his hand to the child, and helping everyone turn the awkward situation into something to laugh about).

A man doesn't become a man overnight. And thusly, women need to be patient, encouraging, and supportive. And the man, also, must be patient with himself. A seven-point rack of antlers doesn't grow upon the brow of a man quickly — it grows throughout a lifetime. But that rack can start growing today.

Here's to the return of the warrior poet!

day twenty-three

MEN III

Men.

The Bible terms them the head of the home. And that term "head" has been abused, in marriages all over the globe, possibly more than any other term in the Bible.

And to be honest, I don't blame women for being a little gun shy when it comes to such a notion. "Head" to many women translates "the abuser," or "the wife-beater," or "the self-centered egotist."

But think about this.

The Bible also says that Jesus is the Head of the Church, which means He is the Authority over all those that believe and trust in Him. And whereas some of the men who have quoted the Bible on this point haven't done such a good job living it out, Jesus did do an amazing job living out His role as Head. He was everything His Bride needed. He was stout, lionhearted, marked by courage, daring, and valor. He was self-sacrificing, merciful, patient, long-suffering, forgiving. He was loving, gentle, kind, courteous, honest, faithful, and true. Long and short, He was everything a head should be.

Jesus loved and still does love His Bride well. And it

says in the Bible that men are supposed to love their wives as Jesus loved the Church.

Well, that's a pretty lofty form of love that a man is supposed to be showing towards his bride, isn't it?

You see, being the head is not what it seems. It's not some position of royalty and luxury. It is not the position of the privileged, but rather it is the position of the sufferer.

Whoever is head is the one who takes the blow, the one who takes the hit. When something goes awry in the home, the head takes the blame.

In a football game, the quarterback will take the onus upon himself if the team loses. It might have been a defensive collapse, but a great quarterback will find a way to take the blame for the loss. That's what the head does. He's responsible for all those under his care.

The head is not a slacker. The head is not a lounger. The head does not get to do what he wants to do, but he does what others like to do. The head will go without food so that others might eat. The head will go cold so that others might be warmed. The head will miss the football game so that his bride can just have a listening ear. The head will miss his hunting trip if something of godly priority comes up.

You see, the concept of headship has gotten all mixed up in our day and age and needs to be straightened back out.

The old-fashioned understanding of a man is that he is the first sufferer. He's the first to experience pain, he's the first to suffer loss, he's the first to stroll onto the battlefield, he's the first to carry his cross, and the first to die upon it.

The first sufferer is Jesus. And the first sufferer is every man fashioned after Christ's noble pattern of leadership.

Here's to changing the stereotype one head at a time.

day twenty-four

THE OLD-FASHIONED GIRL

The Bible uses a term that has caused much debate over the years.

The weaker vessel.

The term itself is harmless; it's that this term in the Bible is associated with women that causes all the fuss.

But, before we initiate the socially sensitive backlash, let's first understand what this idea means.

In a home, children would be considered the weaker vessels. This isn't a criticism of children, a devaluing of them, or a hurtful statement against them. It is merely a statement of fact. For children are in such a manner and, for their proper development, they need to be watched over with great care and concern. They are entrusted to parents (stronger vessels) to help protect them from all unhealthy influences.

In a home, the stronger vessels (the parents) are commissioned to, if necessary, lay down their lives for the weaker vessels (the children). That's only right and proper. In fact, is it not a violation of all that is good and noble, in the midst of danger and attack, for parents to shove their child in front of them and allow him to be harmed in their place?

In a marriage, the Bible clarifies that women are the weaker vessel. Again, like the illustration above, this isn't a criticism of women, a devaluing of them, or a hurtful statement against them. It's merely a statement of fact. And all that is proper and right defends this, even in the realm of natural law. For is it not a violation of all that is good and noble, in the midst of danger and attack, for a husband to shove his wife in front of him and allow her to be harmed in his place?

It may sound old-fashioned to say that a woman is the weaker vessel and that the man should thusly protect her, but that's just the way it is. And, ironically, it's not a statement that devalues a woman, but one that increases her value. For that which is delicate is most prized in God's Kingdom. Little children are precious to Jesus. And, likewise, so are women.

I recognize that there are many women in the world today that are tough as nails and could take me down and stick me in a full nelson in a matter of seconds. This isn't about capability. This isn't about muscle and the art of war. This isn't about intellect. This is about God's ways.

For a woman to be a woman she needs to be strong. But this strength is meant to be wielded in a completely different way than she often expects. She is intended by God to direct her strength, not towards the show of her own attributes, but towards the service of her man. She backs her man's manliness with all the feminine gusto she possesses. And, instead of taking the lead, she holds back. Instead of bullying forward and defending herself, she allows herself to be helped, even rescued.

An old-fashioned girl is rescuable. She allows a man to assist her. She allows a man to be manly and to take the lead. And she cherishes true manliness as if it were the great hope of her day — which it just might be.

An old-fashioned girl doesn't mind one bit the term weaker vessel. For to her it is nothing more than a reminder that her heavenly Bridegroom is the stronger vessel, and she has full confidence in His Almighty rescuing power.

Here's to the return of the old-fashioned girl.

day twenty-five

FLOSSING WITH EXCELLENCE

Hudson, my seven-year-old, went to the dentist yesterday. And he caught the vision for flossing his teeth. So, upon waking up this morning, he ran into the bathroom, whipped out his cinnamon floss, and polished his twenty-two teeth (he knows every one of them). Then at breakfast he asked me if he might floss again after breakfast, in order to make sure his teeth are kept shiny and cavity free. I told him he definitely could. And at this rate he probably will floss upwards of ten times today.

Most of us would probably agree that flossing ten times a day is a bit overboard. However, sometimes we need to be willing to go overboard — we need to follow the drive for excellence in order to find that higher peak of success. For though it may be true that your teeth won't rot if you only floss once a day (or, for that matter, even once a week), what if the goal of oral hygiene changed? What if the great goal of tooth cleaning changed from simply avoiding plaque build-up, to having the brightest, most radiant smile on earth? What if the end game became a positive rather than a negative?

When you change the end game, you change the entire journey and thusly the entire approach.

Most of us are attempting to keep the plaque out of our romantic lives and, therefore, we floss. But we do it almost as a form of duty and we do it at the lowest level of exertion required. It's a fear of dental rot that motivates us, and not the anticipation of the world's most beautiful smile.

But, few of us have caught the vision for having a romance that sparkles with heaven's glow — that glimmers with an otherworldly radiance. So, as a result, we tend only to do what is necessary to not rot, but do nothing in order to see a greater glow.

There are things that each of us can be doing today to be more excellent in our behavior tomorrow. And the same is true for romance. There are things that can be honed, built, and established today in our practical behavior that will cause us to be amazing in our future marriages.

If your love life was a garden, then you would need to learn not to just pull the weeds out, but to plant the flowers in.

As a parent, I desire to see Hudson go far beyond me. Since he is the oldest of my six very lively kiddos, he's become my guinea pig in many ways. You see, I believe that a young boy can be raised, from the beginning, with an attitude of respect and honor. I believe he can start practicing now to be excellent in his future marriage. And I tell him as much.

We actually sit down and have Daddy-Hudson practice sessions. I give him a situation where honor and nobility is required of a man, and I ask him how he would handle it. If he gives the wrong answer, I gently direct him towards the right and honorable course. So, in our home, old-fashioned honor is a very real and present day concept. And a fun one. We laugh a lot about these things. And Leslie and I find no greater delight than to see our little ones showing honor and valor, even if it is in its imperfect form.

I'm convinced God is just the same. He knows that we are infantile in our understanding, but He delights in seeing the little miniature steps of obedience we take.

In the process of training little Hudson, I put together a really fun marriage readiness checklist for him. These are things that I feel, as his father, he should be demonstrating consistently in his life if he is to be ready for marriage. And these are things that he, even at the age of seven, can be practicing now. Some of the things on the list are outright hilarious, while others are straight-faced serious. But they all are deeply significant in their own unique way.

In the next little stretch of this book I'm going to introduce you to the practical things you can begin to do now in order to be made excellent for marriage. Basically, I'm giving you a big spool of floss and I'm saying don't just do the bare minimum required — exert all your energy to do this right. If you are interested in moving beyond the commonplace love story and would like to begin to sharpen your lifestyle, behavior, and actions, then these upcoming twelve days are going to be a lot of fun.

Remember, greatness in marriage is not an accident; it is very purposeful.

Here's to doing this 100% right!

day twenty-six

SHOW A LITTLE RESPECT

I travel quite a bit. And I've just begun to take Hudson with me as I travel. But before he could go on world journeys with Daddy, he first had to pass a test.

He had to show consistent obedience and excellence in a whole host of different areas. For instance, his bed had to be made daily, he had to learn to brush his teeth and shower first thing when he wakes up, he couldn't complain about the food set before him, he had to demonstrate a proper control over his bodily functions and eliminate all "gross habits," and he had to demonstrate that when he saw something needing to be done, he did it without even being asked.

Now I can't say he has proven these things at a level of 100% consistency, but he definitely has shown me a surprising degree of diligence. So, on a recent trip to New York, he came along. It was a big deal. He was a little man on a business trip, and it was fun to watch him rise to the occasion.

Consistency is a key evaluator in this whole romantic schematic. Hudson may make his bed once, but it's the daily discipline that marks him as ready for a trip to New York. The same is true with you. It's not just a burst of eagerness to live pure, right, and set apart that makes you fit for marriage, but the consistent, day in and day out living of honor.

Marriage is a big thing. And it is not to be taken lightly. Therefore, it is critical you start considering your consistency.

Honor, as mentioned earlier, is love in action. It's love in thought, love in deed, and love in attitude. Simply put, it's the practical behavior of Jesus. Or, it could be said, it's what Jesus would be doing if He were the One in that situation instead of you.

A great romance hinges upon the dovetailing of honor and consistency. For when those two fabulous qualities wed inside a man and a woman, then a wedding between that man and woman makes sense.

So, the first evaluation point on our readiness checklist would be exactly that.

Are you consistently demonstrating honor in your life, in your thoughts, in your attitudes, and in your actions?

The great building block of honor is respect. It's considering others as more important than yourself. So, when you are showing honor, it is because you are living in a manner that demonstrates respect and shows value to those around you.

Is respect the essence of your life and behavior? If God were evaluating you to see if you were ready for marriage, do you think He would be giving a big thumbs up right now?

day twenty-seven

PRACTICAL HONOR

So, what does honor look like practically in our lives today, even when we are still single?

Surprisingly, the issues of honor trace to every singular dimension of our lives. But let's look at just a few of those life issues and ratchet up our honor levels in regards to each of them. For, to be excellent in marriage, we need to be excellent in honor.

Clothing

Few of us consider the fact that how we dress makes a statement. It says something about us. And it says something to others about our level of respect for them. When we wear revealing clothing or simply less clothing, we presume that others are interested in seeing our body, and it can often create difficulty for others that are attempting to mind their own business and maintain a purity of thought and life. Even loud clothing can be a distraction. It hollers out, "Hey, look at me — I'm the most important thing in the room." Clothing can also say, "I respect you." When you dress nicely and wear clean and pressed clothes, it says, "You are important enough to me that I would take the time to look good." It may seem strange, but your clothing choices now are setting a pattern for your future marriage. An honorable marriage is marked by two individuals who always look good for each other without creating a noisy distraction for someone else's marriage.

Vocabulary

Your every word spoken needs to be weighed. Crass, crude, and blasphemous words show a high level of disrespect to those around you. They muddy an atmosphere and make others feel awkward. Meanwhile, words of life, gratitude, encouragement, and consideration lend a great deal to the beauty of any environment. If you learn to speak gracious words now, then your marriage will become a beautiful environment.

Gross Habits

How an individual handles his body goes a long way to defining his honorable nature. For instance, when a person sticks a probing finger into their nose, they are showing a disregard to those around them, for such a behavior is revolting to most people on earth (even though they themselves may do the same when no one is looking). But gross habits must be removed wholly and completely. Burping, scratching, making unseemly noises, popping knuckles, and not lifting the toilet seat (yes, that's a man thing) are just a few of the gross habits that top the list. Everything gross should be thrown overboard now, so that everything noble, charming, chivalrous, and excellent has room to maneuver in your love story.

Eye Contact

If you respect someone, you give them eye contact when they are talking to you. You acknowledge what they are saying and show interest. Practice this now and your spouse will certainly appreciate it.

Humor

Unsavory humor is disrespectful to others. Though some may love it, it is indecent, lacking dignity, and wholly absent of honor. Humor itself is a wonderful thing, but humor doesn't have to be off-colored in order to be humorous. A laughing marriage is a great marriage, but crudeness stultifies beauty, like adding trash to a flowery meadow. Keep the laughter around; just get rid of the trash.

Edification

Every word spoken should build up others and never tear down. The gossiping tongue is outrageously dishonoring to everyone involved in the flitting dialogue. It draws others into dishonoring behavior and at the same time is harming someone else not present in the conversation. A spouse will only be intimate to the level they trust your tongue. If they sense that their secrets are not held, then they will cease sharing secrets. Secret-keeping, promise-protecting, and reputation-preserving are the great hallmarks of those who have the delights of intimate love.

Sleep

How you sleep now is how you are preparing to sleep later. And you must realize now that your bed will one day be shared with someone else. Someone who you preferably not kick, elbow, and rudely toss out onto the floor in the middle of the night. Therefore, you must learn how to sleep with calm and order. You must learn to sleep in a manner that honors others. If you snore, then you ought to seek a bodily position which does not encourage snoring. If you hog covers by excessive rolling, then you ought to train yourself how to sleep still in one position and only turn slightly, and without great drama, during the night. To properly be prepared for marriage you must be a respectful sleeper.

Old-fashioned romance must have honor. Without it, the beauty fades, the romance drifts, and the dignity dissipates.

Here's to learning how to not toss our future lover out onto the floor in the middle of the night.

BEWARE THE OVERS

Beware of the Overs. The Overs are like the hole in the love boat. In no time at all they can sink an otherwise wonderful love story.

The Overs exist as a lack of discipline, a looseness of manner, and an acceptance of subtle compromises. So, if you struggle with the Overs, it's high-time that you allow God to sharpen you for excellence.

On the checklist for marriage readiness, this is crucial. So, ponder your answer to the following question:

Are you demonstrating a disciplined manner — not trifling with petty things, but utilizing every moment for the glory of Jesus Christ?

Remember, this is a test of readiness for marriage, so we must take it seriously.

The snooze button is the classic symbol of the Overs. When the snooze button beckons you to push it instead of get up out of bed and start your day, how do you respond? For how you respond to the snooze button is likely how you are responding to the rest of the other "beckonings" throughout the day.

Are you demonstrating a disciplined manner?

The snooze button always has a great argument as to why you should heed it. Overs always do. After all, you worked hard last night and ten more minutes of sleep is only appropriate. However, if that ten more minutes of sleep robs from your ability to do the other things in your morning that are necessary to you being excellent and honorable in your lifestyle, then that would be called Over-sleeping.

If the snooze button rules your mornings now, then it's likely that some of the other Overs are also ruling the other dimensions of your day. And things need to change. For the "Overs" cripple a marriage.

Whereas the snooze button beckons toward Over-sleeping, the all-you-can-eat buffet can beckon you toward Over-eating. But beware of anything and everything in the Over family of vice: Over-playing, Over-spending, Over-resting, Over-talking, Over-reading, Over-meditating on things that are not center and not edifying, and Over-spending on things that are non-essential.

If you wanted to give your future spouse a great gift then go ahead and dump all the Overs over the side of the love boat.

The reason it is such a gift to dump the Overs is because Overs rob from things more important. Too much sleep steals from time with God, time of prayer, and time of study. Too much playing steals time from serving, giving, and ministering to those in need. Too much talking steals from someone else's ability to contribute to the conversation. And too much spending steals from what might be used in a more profitable and life-giving way.

For those of you more loosely inclined, the idea of removing all the Overs might sound a bit overwhelming. But really, it's only hard at first. Because once you walk through the initial transition out of sluggishness and into greater discipline and focus, you actually feel more alive, more free, more able, and you will never want to go back to lying comatose on the couch with a bag of potato chips in your lap.

Here's to cutting ties with all the Overs and their many relatives.

SQUEAKY CLEAN

Have you ever heard it said that God does everything decently and in order?

Well, He does. Just study the periodic table of elements and you are certainly going to stand amazed at God's orderly pattern.

In His creation there is a place for everything. In every eco-system He crafted, He made it to function with an enchanting inter-dependency, He made it to stay pure and clean, and He made it to reflect His nature.

And this cleanliness and orderliness of God brings me to the next question on the marriage readiness checklist:

Are you consistently living a clean and orderly life?

When you are ready for marriage, you will have learned to keep things in order. You will have learned to keep things clean and tidy — whether it's your house, your dorm room, your desk, or merely just your body. And by doing this, you will be demonstrating that your God is a God of cleanliness, light, order, and purity.

Our most primitive practice ground for this idea is in the proper handling of our own personal space.

Here's a quick look at seven-year-old Hudson's

responsibilities, as detailed by Daddy:

Hudson, your bed should always be kept neat. And if it gets ruffled in the night, then first thing in the morning it should be groomed with great attention to detail — not one wrinkle, sheets, blankets, and comforters evenly distributed over the bed, and crisply presented to anyone who might have occasion to see it during the day. And if at all possible, to avoid the build-up of dirt upon the sheets, you must be watchful to ensure that your sheets are washed and freshened weekly.

You must determine a place for everything — clean clothes, dirty clothes, toys, books, pencils, pens, extra change, etc. And once you determine the place for these things, then you must make sure that these things, though they be used during the day, are always immediately put back into their proper place after use. This will help to ensure a tidy environment and thus lay a healthy foundation for a tidy marriage and a tidy family in the future.

I don't think most people understand how significant these things are in marriage. But, a spouse that lofts underwear onto the floor, leaves the bed a wrinkled mess in the morning, and keeps junk lying around to be picked up at a later date is not a spouse who is going to enjoy the ongoing loveliness and wonder of marriage intimacy. For order and cleanliness has a great effect on the desire for closeness.

But it's not just the room that needs picking up and polishing; it's also the body.

Here's my exhortation to Hudson on the matter:

Hudson, you also must learn to keep your body in order, healthy, clean, and fresh smelling. You must learn to make sure your mouth is always kept fresh, with frequent tooth brushings and periodic mouthwash. You should wear deodorant in order that your personal smell not overpower any given environment. You should bathe daily, or as frequently as possible, in order to maintain a cleanness to your body and a freshness to your bearing. You should groom your hair to make sure that it does not prove a distraction but only an enhancement to your life conversation. And you should always dress in clothing that is appropriate for the situation, clean and pressed, in order that your bearing might be respectful to those you encounter in your journeys.

Do these things matter in marriage? You better believe it they do. For cleanliness is a means of showing respect and love to your spouse. For most people don't want to kiss a gorilla, cuddle with a pig, or sleep next to a hippo. They desire a member of the opposite sex that is clean and fresh smelling. And, it is important to note that a future spouse will undoubtedly find great satisfaction in this "clean and orderly" pattern of behavior. But beware — for you will surely be overwhelmed in your marriage with a multitude of hugs, kisses, and cuddles (from your spouse, of course) as a result of such attention to detail.

Here's to being overwhelmed with hugs, kisses, and cuddles.

THOUGHTFULNESS

Have you ever heard it said that "romance dies after the honeymoon"?

I've always bristled at that statement. The statement lacks hope and it offends an innate desire within me to see married love succeed, to see intimacy continue on, and on, and on.

I personally believe that romance doesn't need to die after the honeymoon. But, that said, I fully understand why it does in many situations. It's because thoughtfulness was never cultivated as a consistent character quality prior to the inception of the love story. Don't worry — I'll explain.

Thoughtfulness is the operative word for today.

It's certainly not a flowery word or a big-personality word at all. Rather, it's a humble, blue-collar sort of word that everyone knows as nice and socially pleasant, but most overlook when the likes of sex, intimacy, romance, closeness, pleasure, and affection are also in the room with all their glitz and glamorous appeal.

Certain words have cache value. Thoughtfulness doesn't. However, when you get a bit more familiar with it, you will realize that it is anything but plain. It's just quietly extraordinary in its romantic powers.

First, let's define what thoughtfulness even is. In the most basic sense, it means being "full of thought" for someone else other than yourself. It means thinking of others and of doing them good throughout your day. It's pondering practical ways that your life might offer strength, pleasure, and assistance to others.

Thoughtfulness is not rocket science; it's just Christianity.

But strangely, thoughtfulness doesn't come naturally to any of us. We can esteem it, but that doesn't mean we do it. And it's not that we don't care about others; it's that we usually don't think about others until they are standing right in front of us.

You see, for a man and woman to see romance continue onward even after the honeymoon, they need to have a cultivated and practiced foundation in thoughtfulness. Because, whether it is noticed or not, romance is merely the shining armor on the venerable knight known as Thoughtful.

What most people call romance is just thoughtfulness applied in an affectionate and beautiful manner towards a lover.

When someone is falling in love they are "full of thought" towards the one they adore. It is easy to remember them. Love is on their mind. And therefore things like flowers, cards, poems, and planning romantic interludes flow unhindered. In the falling in love season, thoughtfulness seems easy, romance comes naturally, and kisses, sweet nothings, and tender embraces are never far away. All seems so blissful, but it's because of all the thought being given. What no one is expecting is that after the heart is won, the vows exchanged, and the honeymoon complete, the thoughts don't come as easily. And if a lover never learned to be thoughtful as a way of life, prior to his romantic pursuits, then he will not have the romantic skills in place to succeed in keeping the romance strong in marriage.

And this is precisely why this must go on our checklist for marriage readiness:

Are you proving a thoughtful person?

For if you can learn right now how to be the venerable knight, Thoughtful — even when it is not for romantic purposes — then you will be ready to don the shining armor when the day of romance comes and never see the beauty dwindle even after the honeymoon ends.

Thoughtfulness can be practiced in many ways, but I would like to mention two very specific ways that could greatly enhance your effectiveness in your future love story.

1) IN THE CULTIVATION OF PROPER HEAVENLY MANNERS

For instance, appropriately saying "thank you" after something generous is done for you. Looking people in the eye when they talk with you and giving them undivided focused attention. Eating the food that is set before you without complaint, but with gladness no matter what manner of food it is. Showing proper table manners and, when done, always seeking ways to help clean up both your own plate and the plates of everyone around you. Opening the door for girls, talking with a respectful and quieter volume in a public place, and always showing deference to the elders among you. These might not seem romantic in nature, and that is because they aren't. The secret to romance isn't romance; it's what lies beneath — what motivates the kind and noble act.

When you are ready for marriage, you will consistently demonstrate that you have eyes to see the needs of those around you. And this must be constantly practiced. Every day in every situation, you should learn to ask God the question, "Is there anyone I can be of service to right now?" Most people spend all their time thinking about how they can serve themselves. But not you. You should be interested in becoming a benefit to the lives of everyone around you. So, you should demonstrate this in a thousand and one different ways. If you see the kitchen garbage filling up, you should figure out where it needs to go and take out the trash. If you see that the toilet paper roll is out, you should hunt down a replacement. If you notice the floor needs sweeping, the dishes need washing, or a light bulb needs changing, you shouldn't wait to be asked to help — you should just jump up and get the job done. For if you can learn to jump up and tend to these small things, you will then be prepared to jump up and tend to the needs in your marriage in the future.

But it is important to note that thoughtfulness is not just for practical fix-it or clean-up things around the house. You should also know how to show expressions of thoughtful warmth and affection to those in your range of relationship. You should enjoy bringing surprises that kindle notions of love and appreciation — a note written, a picture drawn, a poem left, a flower strategically laid, or a thousand other things beside. You should prove thoughtful in your younger years, for if you do, you will never lose your thoughtfulness in your elder years.

2) IN LEARNING TO TREAT PARENTS AND SIBLINGS AS ROYALTY

Many romantics-in-training will be on their very best behavior when on a date. They will do noble things, speak gently, act kindly, and even open doors and pay checks. But upon their arrival home, they are nightmares toward everyone living under their same roof. They are wholly inconsistent. They are thoughtful when it benefits themselves, but then wholly selfish when it doesn't.

This is a very dangerous trend and must be remedied. For as my mom once rightly declared, "Eric, the way you treat me is the way you are going to treat your future spouse."

We are setting patterns in place now in our first family that are certain to carry over into our next family. And for many of us those patterns are not very healthy.

So, as a matter of principle, you will be ready for marriage only when you have learned to treat others as more important than yourself. But, out of all the people on earth, you should learn to show an extra special courtesy, honor, deference, and thoughtfulness towards your God-given family members. You should speak of their strengths and avoid ever needing to mention their frailties. You should serve them in any way you can, pray for them always, seek their protection, and always yearn for their health, security, and spiritual maturity. When you learn to be excellent in your relationship with your parents and siblings, then you will, as a matter of course, be excellent in your future marriage.

Thoughtfulness practiced now on the likes of friends and family members might not be deemed romantic. But, I can assure you, it will prove the lifelong underlayment for a romance that will never die.

Here's to a romance that only grows more beautiful after the honeymoon.

MONEY

Money.

It seems rather harmless when you open up your wallet. But those dollars and cents have proven the undoing of more than a few marriages down through the years.

Money is sort of like fire. If it is kept in its proper context, stoked and tended with excellence, then it warms the entire house and adds beauty to the environment. However, if it gets outside of its rightful place (a.k.a. the fireplace), then it burns down the entire house.

Money has a place in our lives, in our home, and in our marriages. But it mustn't get outside that place. It mustn't become what our lives are about. It mustn't be the key defining factor in all our decision-making.

For instance, if you marry someone because of their wealth, then you have let the fire out of its proper context. If you believe that marriage can only be happy when money is superfluous, then you will certainly never find happiness, for the fire is out of its place.

Technically, money isn't what burns down a marriage. It's the love of the stuff that get us. And you don't have to be wealthy to love money. The poorest of the poor can lose their marriages over the love of money as well.

Most of us think that we have to have a lot of money to be happy. But you can have a lot of money and have a miserable marriage. And, amazingly, you can have none of it and have a great marriage. The presence of money is not what makes a marriage great. And, likewise, the absence of money is not what makes a marriage great.

But, rightly handling money and being skilled at dealing with dollars and cents can prove a significant tool in a world-class marriage.

So, let's add this to the checklist for marriage readiness. Are you handling money or is money handling you?

When you are ready for marriage you will demonstrate a seriousness about not letting money get the better of you or your future marriage. You must not be controlled by money, led by the need for money, or overly-fascinated with the idea of getting more money.

Money must not be treated as the enemy, but it also must not be treated as the solution to life's problems. Jesus is the solution and will always be the solution. More of Jesus is what causes life to work and not just more money. However, money plays an important role in the success of a great marriage, because, in a certain way, money is necessary to the function of life on earth. We all need it, but we don't need to be controlled by our need for it. And we all will have it, but money does not need to have us. The way in which you learn to handle it will define, in a large degree, the atmosphere of your future marriage and family. So, it's critical that you learn how to utilize money properly.

In the Bible, there is a simple rule of thumb for

approaching the issue of money:

Seek the priority of Jesus first in your life.

Receive your assignment from Him.

And then let God back you up with the necessary resources to pull off the assignment.

The Bible certainly does not support laziness. Quite the contrary, it commands a diligent work ethic. But it doesn't commission us to seek money with our work ethic, but rather to seek Jesus.

In other words, someone who trusts in Jesus can be completely 100% confident that God will supply the money if they direct their diligence and work ethic straight towards the glory of the King of kings.

And then, when the money is supplied by God, there is another rule of thumb for how to properly utilize the money that God gives:

Splurge on the Sacred Things.

Skimp on the Secular Things.

Starve the Profane Things.

Splurging on the sacred things means spending freely on the things that express His Kingdom, that build up lives, and that showcase Gospel love.

Skimping on things that are secular means cautious spending on the things that are not central and that do not represent Jesus's priority here on earth (i.e. things like fancy cars, yachts, and other royal toys).

And then starving the things that are profane means not spending even one dime on anything that is polluted, perverted, or contrary to the purposes of our King here on earth.

If you can begin today to extravagantly spend your resources on the things that matter most and, meanwhile, prove miserly towards everything else — then when it comes to marriage, you will give your all towards that which builds your marriage stronger and you will starve all those things which seek to make your marriage weaker.

Here's to keeping money in its place.

day thirty-two

FAITHFULNESS

When growing up I always thought I would get married someday. But, in my mind, this "person" whom I would one day marry wasn't actually a real person. She was a concept, an idea. In other words, my future spouse didn't actually live, breathe, and have a hair color.

Now, I wouldn't have said such a thing back then. I don't know if I actually even fully understood my own thoughts on the matter. But that is essentially the case. My someday girl was nothing more than a thought.

I'll never forget the day in college, while thinking about this someday girl, when I suddenly had a flash. It was an awakening, an epiphany. I realized that my future spouse wasn't a concept, or an idea — she was an actual person. And, she was alive!

I know it sounds utterly bizarre to say I didn't understand that until college, but, honestly, I didn't. And, as a result, I hadn't been living as if my future spouse was an actual person. I hadn't lived as if she was alive.

Little did I know that I was stumbling upon one of the most important qualities of a beautiful lifelong romance. It was like seeing a shimmer of gold in a rock wall of granite. So, I took out my chisel and went after the gold.

What I found was the idea of faithfulness.

Faithfulness to me had always been a concept wholly reserved for marriage. After all, how can someone be faithful if he hasn't even yet met the person he is going to marry? But that was the point. Faithfulness is living in such a way as to honor the good trust of another.

My future spouse desired me to be kept, to be hers and only hers. And yet, when I looked at my life and I asked myself if I was honoring her good trust, the answer was no.

If she were to somehow be able to see me interacting with other girls, the question suddenly floating through my mind was, "Would she feel loved?" If she were to see me flirting and attempting to grab the affections of other girls, I suddenly had the realization that she would feel threatened. If she were to see me romantically entwined with someone else, then I would be guilty of sponsoring jealousy within her heart.

This got me thinking.

I began to realize that my future wife cares. She has feelings. She has longings. She has a defined way that she would want me to be living right now.

It was an odd thought, but a revolutionary one.

My thought was, "What if I began to be a one-woman man, starting right now?"

What if I were to start being faithful to her even before I meet her?

What if I were to actually treat her like my princess starting today?

You see, this belongs on our checklist for marriage readiness:

Are you practicing faithfulness right now towards your

future spouse?

I've always referred to this as "the two eyeball principle." Leslie has never liked my name for it, but it's a good name. I always imagined two eyeballs floating in the air about six inches above my left shoulder. They belonged to my future spouse, and they could see everything I was doing. And I decided that if she were going to be watching me, I wanted to live in such a way that she would feel honored and cherished.

Life changes quite dramatically if you begin to live as if you are "taken." And I was now "taken." I wasn't on the open market — there was one girl out there, who I still hadn't met, who held my heart.

It was faithfulness even before the first "hello."

And here's the amazing thing about learning faithfulness right now, even before you meet your someday boy or girl: if you learn it now, you will always have it.

It's sort of like learning how to drive a stick shift. Once you get it down, you just sort of always have it down. It's the behavior pattern of loyalty. And right now is the best day to begin practicing it.

I used to pray for my girl every night and I used to write her love notes. And I'll never forget how amazing it was when I presented a notebook full of love letters to her on our honeymoon — some of them written years before I ever even met her. Oh, the bliss of doing it the old-fashioned way.

Here's to beginning to put together your very own notebook of love letters.

A KISS

A kiss.

There's nothing quite like a good old-fashioned kiss. It's tender, romantic, chivalrous, and full of authentic affection.

But Hollywood has introduced a ridiculous substitute for the true kissing art. We could call it the animalistic kiss — you know, the open mouth, saliva-strewn extravaganza.

You can witness a good old-fashioned sort of kiss and not blush with shame. It's sweet, pure, and noble. But not the Dracula kind. It forces you to look away. And to be quite frank, it's not in any way beautiful. It's forceful, harsh, and demeaning. It's like a race through the botanical gardens to reach the water fountain, missing the lush flowery and fragrant beauty along the way.

The physical dimension of a relationship is wonderful. But the old-fashioned code of honor demands that it be handled with great care and sacred timing.

A kiss is amazing. But a saved kiss is even more amazing.

God has created a context in which physical touch is supposed to be enjoyed. And that is inside the safe confines of covenant commitment. When sacred touches are enjoyed outside this sacred commitment, it's not that they don't have any enjoyment value — they do. But it is a temporary pleasure. Its beauty wanes and something more exotic and exciting must then fill the hole. But when a sacred touch is enjoyed in the safety of sacred commitment, it never dulls, it never grows tiresome — but rather, always maintains its hue of enchantment.

An old-fashioned romance guards the physical dimension of the relationship. It keeps sacred touches reserved for sacred moments and then enjoys them in a sacred fashion.

Leslie and I made a strange decision in our generation. We decided to save our first kiss until our wedding day.

A kiss to us had lost its regality. For both of us, the tender simplicity and pure affection of a kiss had eroded away. And we wanted to get it back.

One of our inspirations for this was Leslie's great-grandmother. As the story goes, in the horse-drawn carriage on the way to her wedding ceremony, her husband-to-be leaned over and attempted to kiss her on the cheek. She slapped him and muttered, "There will be plenty of time for that after the wedding!"

Leslie and I joked about that often as we were navigating this arena. And, to be quite honest, it wasn't easy. It is never easy to restrain touch. But good things do come to those who wait.

What Leslie and I found was that a simple kiss, when waited for, becomes something so much more. It becomes a sacred symbol of love, a token of commitment. And a kiss waited for is a kiss fully enjoyed. And amazingly, a kiss, when placed in its proper sacred context, will never lose its luster, but will always be held precious and dear.

Many people think of physical purity as following a drab and legalistic code. But, it's anything but that. It's a statement from one lover to another that they want to do whatever it takes to secure the highest degrees of beauty in their marriage.

What would you be willing to do to gain the pinnacle of beauty in your future marriage?

No one promised it would be easy. But I can assure you it would be worth it.

So, let's add this to our checklist for marriage readiness:

Are you saving sacred touches for sacred moments?

Here's to kisses the way kisses were originally intended to be!

day thirty-four

INSPIRATION FOR PRACTICAL RENOVATION

Is anyone ever really ready for marriage?

That's a great question.

It would certainly be true that everyone who says "I do" could be more ready than they are at that moment. However, there seem to be certain things that, if in place, will enable someone to move forward in marriage without a kerfuffle of unnecessary challenges.

Note the word "unnecessary" in the previous sentence. You see, there are necessary challenges that come with the territory of an ever-growing relationship, and it is not those we are trying to avoid. It's all the unnecessary stuff we want to circumvent.

So, to avoid all that unnecessary conflict, we've been building a short checklist to help you with discerning your marriage readiness. Let's look at the six questions of evaluation we have on our list:

Are you demonstrating a disciplined lifestyle?

Are you consistently living a clean and orderly life?

Are you proving a thoughtful person?

Are you handling money or is money handling you?

Are you practicing faithfulness right now towards your future spouse?

Are you saving sacred touches for sacred moments?

This is great stuff. And when put into practice, it produces great results.

There are many more things we could add to this list. There is a myriad of items any marriage could benefit from, but the point is to focus on things we can begin to practice right now in order to ensure a world-class marriage someday in the future.

If I was going to add a few bonus questions that would hearken back to the real heart of old-fashioned romance, here's my short list:

Is God holding the pen and fully allowed to write your love story?

Is God the center of your every day? Can your life be summarized in the fact that you are in a great pursuit to know God more?

Are you proving to be the first sufferer?

Are you demonstrating that you are quick to sacrifice for the benefit of others? Are you willing to go without so that others may have? Are you giving up your strength for the benefit of those that are weak?

Are you proving to be forgiving and forgivable?

Are you quick to forgive those who hurt you and are you ensuring that, before you go to bed each night, you've made right all that was made wrong during your day? Are you quick to offer forgiveness when it is sought of you?

Are you investing now in being the ultimate spouse tomorrow?

Are you taking every opportunity to be refined and to grow up as a follower of Jesus? Are you cultivating skills that would serve well in making your future home stronger (i.e. cooking, handyman skills, sewing, auto-mechanical, electrical, typing, fine carpentry, etc.)? And are you eating your vegetables — in other words, are you taking care of the body that you are soon to be giving in marriage?

It is not perfection that marriage demands — just a perfect response to all our imperfections along the way. None of us are going to be without flaw; however, we have the God who is without flaw, and He is willing to move into our bodies and make our life work from the inside out.

If we allow Him in, He will take our otherwise pitiful lives and make them sparkle with His majesty.

Here's to being made excellent for marriage!

HEAVEN COME TO EARTH

What is marriage anyway?

After all, that's really what this book is all about. For if two people walk in honor, purity, and old-fashioned excellence in their romance, then wedding bells eventually chime.

Living together is an avoidance of covenant commitment. It's not the right way of doing things. It's not the honorable approach.

Marriage is a sacred act of heavenly grace. And it's more than a contract. It's a holy covenant. It's an exchange. It's a lifetime surrender. It's the choosing of one person for the rest of one's life. It's beautiful, noble, a celebration, a joy, a tribute to the Creator.

It's just plain right.

But what is marriage for?

Is it for decency?

Is it for children?

Is it for God-accepted, legal sex?

Is it for a tax break?

What is it for?

It's for God.

Marriage is about Him.

My goal in my marriage is not to please me. My goal in my marriage is to please God.

My goal in my marriage is not to be served by my wife. My goal in my marriage is to serve my wife.

My goal in my marriage isn't merely to have kids. My goal in my marriage is to properly raise kids who live their lives wholly and fully for Jesus Christ.

Marriage is the end of every God-honoring romance.

But marriage is also just the beginning of every God-honoring romance.

For marriage isn't truly an end. It is a vehicle which carries a love deeper, higher, farther, and beyond.

Marriages built by God get better with time. They don't fall apart after the honeymoon, but rather mature with time, ripen with the trials of life, and become more robust with every passing year. Love deepens. Intimacy heightens. Appreciation grows. And affection multiplies to the point where tears come to your eyes even when you think of that special one who has said no to all others simply to purposely spend their life with you.

Marriage is heaven on earth.

And it is high time that we started protecting it as the sacred cornerstone of every truly honorable and noble society.

Here's to happily ever after.

'TIL DEATH PARTS

One of the classic moments in every wedding ceremony is the exchange of vows.

But a vow has lost its meaning to us in our modern day. It seems to be considered more poetry than promise. However, the "old-fashioned" reason why witnesses were invited to a wedding ceremony was to "witness the covenant" and thusly hold the bride and groom accountable to their vows 'til death part them.

Whether living in plenty or in want.

Whether living in sickness or in health.

Do words like these even matter anymore?

When times get tough, modern lovers move on. They yell out, "I didn't sign up for all this difficulty."

But, technically, they did sign up for all this difficulty.

Old-fashioned love stories are made great by overcoming difficulty. That is their secret.

We have allowed a strange notion to sneak inside our modern concept of love and intimacy, and that is that difficulty is bad.

Well, I agree that difficulty is hard. But difficulty is not bad. In fact, difficulty, when handled correctly, is the great secret to romantic growth and the deepening of intimacy.

An old-fashioned sort of romantic smiles at difficulty, and treats it as his close friend.

The pastor who married Leslie and me was a bit unorthodox in his methods. He handed Leslie and me a legally binding contract and said, "If I'm going to marry you, you have to read this, agree to this, and sign it."

"What is it?" we asked.

He smiled and said, "It says that you cannot get a divorce — that if you have an issue in your marriage, you cannot settle it in a court of law, but you must deal with it through Christian mediation."

I had never heard of such a thing. And Leslie and I sort of looked at each other and said, "Well, we're not planning on ever getting a divorce, so I guess it doesn't matter if we legally declare that it is an impossibility."

It's funny, but Leslie and I have never even considered divorce. First off, it's not an option legally for us. But secondly, it's not an option spiritually for us. If we have a problem, we have found that working through our problems brings us closer. And after seventeen years of marriage, all of our difficulties have only increased our love and affection, not hindered it.

In our modern day, there is a rise of prenuptial agreements that preserve the wealth and intellectual property of the two Hollywood celebrities as they drive off in their Bentley toward their two-million-dollar luxury honeymoon spree on the Riviera. There is a lot of hoopla surrounding their romance, but not a lot of depth or meaning. There is a lot of money, a lot of glamor, and a lot of fireworks, but it's hollow, without noble beauty. It is estranged of any true heart warmth, trust, and affection.

I've never thought about it before, but I guess, in a way, Leslie and I signed a prenuptial agreement. But it wasn't a prenuptial agreement that preserved our things, our fortune, our reputation, and our future independence, but rather it was one that signed it all away — forever and always and ever after.

Difficulties, trials, and tribulations are certain to come. But when they do, are you prepared to embrace them or escape them?

It may seem a bit old-fashioned, but my encouragement to you is to truly declare, from the depths of your soul, "No matter what, 'til death do us part!"

Here's to removing the option of divorce clean off the table of your future!

day thirty-seven

BOUNDARIES

Boundaries.

I realize we are not instinctively attracted to things like boundaries. We want a complete removal of restraint, an unharnessed life.

But the life that works must wear a harness. The romance that works must have boundaries.

Boundaries have received a bad rap in our modern culture. They have officially been classified as "old-fashioned." They are referred to with disgust as repressive and dour. But, actually, they preserve life and help to protect the true beauty and dignity of a relationship.

When I was falling in love with Leslie, her dad played a big role in the unfolding drama. I came to him and I asked him to help me do this whole thing right. And he obliged.

Right near the beginning of the relationship, he said something to me that I'll never forget.

"Eric," he said, "it's the responsibility of the man to seek out the woman's boundaries."

"What do you mean by boundaries?" I questioned.

"I mean, the interaction physically that she feels is

appropriate prior to marriage," he answered. "Every woman has a physical boundary that she has determined to be appropriate physical interaction. And that boundary must never be crossed. It's up to the man to find out what this boundary is and then become the defender of that boundary in their relationship."

But that wasn't all that Leslie's dad said.

"This is very important, Eric," he continued, "because if a man violates that boundary prior to marriage, even if the woman invites him to do so in the heat of passion, she will always resent his lack of protection over her sacred defined line."

Every man wants to be strong for his girl. But what amazed me about this concept is that a man's protection and trustworthiness wasn't defined in how he defended his home after marriage, but in how he preserved his wife's purity prior to marriage.

To kiss or not to kiss is not really the question. The question is whether you are willing to forgo physical pleasure now in order to ensure a greater level of intimacy, trust, and affection in your marriage in the future.

Here's to answering such a question with a big fat "yes!"

day thirty-eight

IS THERE
AN ERASER?

Ever since our book, *When God Writes Your Love Story,* strolled onto the publishing stage back in 1998, we've been challenging lovers everywhere to "give God the pen." And whereas some of you reading this forty-day journey are fine and dandy with giving God the pen to write your story, what you really wish you could do is "give God the eraser" to scratch out the rotten story you have already written.

But God doesn't erase your past mistakes.

This might not sound like good news, but it actually is. Because although He doesn't remove your past mistakes from the story of your life and overwrite them in the history annals with nice, sweet-sounding stories (that actually never happened), He does something even better than erase them.

He takes all the bad things in our past, and, when requested, He turns them into beautiful pictures of His grace. He transforms them. Like little homely caterpillars, He wraps them in the silky cocoon of His gracious redemptive power, and then removes the husk, only to reveal something homely transformed into something beautiful.

The Bible says it this way in Isaiah 61:3...

(He give us) beauty for ashes, the oil of joy for mourning, the garment of praise for the spirit of heaviness.

In fact, God isn't intimidated by your past. For where there is much to forgive, there is much room in which to reveal His great love and grace.

Those who have never stumbled have never had to endure the scrapes and scratches included in the stumbling. So, they are certainly blessed. But those who have never stumbled have also never needed to be helped back up. And there is an intimate blessing that is difficult to describe — that even brings tears to the eyes — that comes from calling out to God in your brokenness and receiving His outstretched hand of mercy.

Every mistake in your past can be turned into a strength in your future.

Every error of bygone days can become a virtue in the days to come.

That's just God's way.

But the key is to ask Him to do it. When the caterpillar refuses to enter the cocoon, the cocoon of redemptive grace is unable to work the transformation. But when the caterpillar is willing... God is more than ready to work a miracle in your love life.

Here's to climbing into that silky cocoon and letting God do what only God can do.

day thirty-nine

WEAKNESS

The content of this book won't save your relationship from certain disaster. Only God can truly make a romance sparkle. So, how you engage with God on this matter is of the utmost significance.

Here you are on your thirty-ninth day, almost at the finish. But if you are still the one in the driver's seat of your life, then even though you are thirty-nine days into this book, you are not even close to being ready to put it down and pick up a brilliant love story.

Only God can make a great lover. And you allowing God to do the "making" is the great central principle of this book. For, in your own self-muscle and willpower, you can do all the right things — even attempt to be Mr. Romantic — but if it's still selfish old you (with all your baggage and junk) lingering in the relationship, it's only a matter of time before the breakdown begins.

I have a word for today that doesn't sound very romantic: **weakness**.

It may not be a triumphant sounding word, but, rightly addressed, it is the key to triumph.

Long and short, we are all very weak and ill-equipped

to do this whole relationship thing right. And without an impetus from outside ourselves, we are doomed to failure.

It's when we understand our weakness that we are able to avail ourselves of Christ's strength.

I simply can't do it right. I can't be pure in my heart and mind. I can't love with selfless givenness. I can't be Mr. Noble. I can't be Mr. Sweet. I can't be thoughtful, faithful, and self-sacrificing. But I know Someone who can be all those things in and through me.

The secret to great and lasting love is rightly understanding weakness. For, no matter how many years we are into this journey, we will still be weak and in need of outside intervention.

If I were on an airplane headed over the Atlantic, there would never be an appropriate time to consider myself able to fly and therefore no longer in need of the airplane. I am simply unable to fly without assistance. And therefore, the secret to my flight is to remain firmly seated inside that airplane. And the same is true in my relationship with Jesus Christ.

Weakness is not an excuse for moral lassitude and moral ambivalence. And weakness is not a creative cover for mediocrity and compromise. Weakness is an important daily reminder that it is not me that makes an old-fashioned romance work. It's Him.

And because I am weak I must not consider myself strong and able to endure temptations. So I flee from temptation, as opposed to declaring, "Oh, watch how strong I am!" There is only One who can navigate me through temptations and He's only useful to me when I recognize how desperately I need Him.

As a result of this inherent weakness, the old-fashioned

lover is watchful over his circumstances. To truly be honorable, he will never put himself or another person into a situation that depends on human grit and restraint to survive. Weakness is remembered, and therefore temptations are to be avoided like the plague. Compromising situations are to be purposely circumvented with great care.

It's old-fashioned, I realize, but remember, that is precisely what this book is all about.

The man who would understand his own weakness and God's great strength is a man fit to not only love a woman well, but to lead nations well.

Here's to embracing weakness and thusly changing the world.

day forty

THE GUEST OF HONOR

When we reach our graying years and we gaze back upon our life, it will be our wedding day, perhaps more than any other day, that we can look to as either the start of something great or the start of something grating.

Christ performed His first miracle on earth while attending a wedding.

Why choose a wedding for such a momentous occasion?

Because a wedding is the perfect enunciation of His great plan. It's a picture of selfless love, binding covenant, sacred generosity, and sacrificial friendship. A wedding is an earthly picture of God's heavenly agenda. God came to earth to rescue His Bride. He came to earth for the purpose of covenanting with the one(s) He loved.

As far as God is concerned, a wedding isn't merely a formality; it is meant to be a demonstration of His Gospel to all those who witness on earth and in the heavenly realms.

It is profoundly beautiful what Christ chose as His very

first miracle. It wasn't something glamorous like raising the dead or giving sight to a blind man. In fact, on the surface His very first miracle seems rather anticlimactic. Many of us often write off His first miracle as something He did to "warm up" for the bigger things to come. But God was making a statement with His first miracle. A statement that none of us should miss.

As the story goes, during the latter stages of this wedding celebration, it came to Christ's attention that there was a shortage on wine. In a Hebrew wedding, this was tantamount to disaster. Jesus asked the servants to fill six enormous stone jars with water, and then he told them to draw some out and take it to the master of the banquet.

When the master of the banquet tasted what was in the glass, he didn't taste water but wine. He called the bridegroom aside and said, "Every man at the beginning sets out the good wine, and when the guests have well drunk, then the inferior. You have kept the good wine until now!" (John 2:10, NKJV).

The model of the world's love brings out the choice wine in the beginning of the celebration, and then from that point on the quality disintegrates. So often young lovers find an electric sensual love in the beginning of their affair only to see it whittle down into a passionless bore as the weeks and months pass. But Christ has a different model, a revolutionary model, which He proved with His very first miracle.

The quality of the celebration, the romance, and the intimacy only gets better with time when He is invited to the wedding and allowed to build the marriage.

When Christ isn't invited to the wedding, the six stone

jars remain unused and no miracle takes place. The sweet wine is used up in the beginning of the romance and the stone jars are unable to fill themselves full of water and transform it into a fine wine.

The difference between a failed wedding and a successful one comes down to one very simple thing — the guest list. Was Christ invited?

If not, the marriage may start out with song and dance, but it ends with disappointment and regret. The wine will run out.

Every day around this world, the stone jars remain empty and the spark of celebratory love fades with the turn of the hour hand on the clock. Christ was not invited to the wedding; He was not asked to fill our stone jars with the ordinary substance of life and transform it into the extraordinary substance of lifelong, ever-growing marital beauty.

When He is made our Guest of honor, the Author of our love story, our wedding Coordinator, and the Testator of our covenant, not only will our celebratory wine never run out, but it will get tastier and tastier as the love story progresses.

This is God's way. He invented married love to be a foretaste of His love. He designed marriage to be an earthly sampling of eternal life in heaven with Him as our Bridegroom. And His version of love, just like fine wine, gets better and better as time passes.

Our future wedding day is not only an opportunity to display these amazing truths of God's kingdom. It is also only the first of a million more opportunities in marriage to showcase the glory of God for this world to see and comprehend His nature.

But don't just wait for your wedding day. I encourage you to set out your life, like the six stone jars, before Christ. Ask Him to fill you full of Himself, the Living Water, and transform your relationship into a miracle that proves that old-fashioned love only gets sweeter and sweeter with the passing of time.

ABOUT THE AUTHOR

There were three things growing up that Eric Ludy declared he would never become: a teacher, a missionary, and a pastor. He became all three. In a vain attempt to gain some credibility he also became a writer. But seventeen books later, he's admitted that this plan backfired big time—the messages contained in his books have led to more scorn than the other three combined. Ludy is the president of Ellerslie Mission Society, the teaching pastor at the Church at Ellerslie, and the lead instructor in the Ellerslie Discipleship Training. He descended from seven generations of pastors, is totally uncool, somewhat skinny, and in Japan supposedly his last name means "nerd." But, that said, he is clothed in the shed blood of His beloved Savior; Leslie, his wife of twenty years, still laughs at his jokes; and his six kids think he is Superman (or at least Clark Kent). So, all is well with the author of this book. He calls Windsor, Colorado home, but longs for his real home in heaven where being a "fool for Christ" finally will be realized to be the most brilliant life-decision any human has ever made.

EricLudy.com

MORE BOOKS FROM ERIC LUDY

Romance, Relationships, & Purity
When God Writes Your Love Story
When Dreams Come True
Meet Mr. Smith
A Perfect Wedding
The First 90 Days of Marriage
Teaching True Love to a Sex-at-13 Generation
It Takes a Gentleman and a Lady

Godly Manhood
God's Gift to Women

Christian Living & Discipleship
When God Writes Your Life Story
The Bravehearted Gospel
Heroism

Prayer
Wrestling Prayer

Memoirs & Confessions
Are These Really My Pants?
Evolution of the Pterodactyl
The Bold Return of the Dunces
Fingerprints of Grace

EricLudy.com

DISCOVER MORE
FROM THE AUTHOR

SERMONS

Unashamed Gospel Thunder.

Listen now: Ellerslie.com/sermons

CONFERENCES

Come expectant. Leave transformed.

Learn more: Ellerslie.com/conferences

DISCIPLESHIP TRAINING

A set apart season to become firmly
planted in Christ.

Learn more: Ellerslie.com/training

READ MORE FROM ERIC LUDY

EricLudy.com

Printed in Great Britain
by Amazon